Tullius C. O'Kane

Joy to the World

Sacred songs for gospel meetings

Tullius C. O'Kane

Joy to the World
Sacred songs for gospel meetings

ISBN/EAN: 9783337265441

Printed in Europe, USA, Canada, Australia, Japan

Cover: Foto ©Lupo / pixelio.de

More available books at **www.hansebooks.com**

Joy to the World:

— OR, —

SACRED SONGS FOR GOSPEL MEETINGS.

— BY —

T. C. O'KANE, C. C. M'CABE,
AND
JNO. R. SWENEY.

HITCHCOCK AND WALDEN,
Cincinnati, Chicago, St. Louis.
NEW YORK: PHILLIPS & HUNT.
1879.

PREFACE.

"*The joy of the Lord is your strength.*"

"*Weeping may endure for a night, but joy cometh in the morning.*"

"*Cry out and shout, thou inhabitant of Zion, for great is the Holy One of Israel in the midst of thee.*"

"*For ye shall go out with joy, and be led forth with peace; the mountains and the hills shall break forth before you into singing, and all the trees of the field shall clap their hands. Instead of the thorn shall come up the fir-tree, and instead of the brier shall come up the myrtle tree: and it shall be to the Lord for a name, for an everlasting sign that shall not be cut off.*"

We send forth this little volume, freighted with song, trusting that in the Social Meetings, in the Revivals and Camp-meetings of the Church, in the Sabbath-schools and at the Family Altars, it may prove a

JOY TO THE WORLD!

in contributing something towards filling the earth with the melody of that name

"*That charms our fears,
And bids our sorrows cease—
'Tis music in the sinner's ears,
'Tis life and health and peace.*"

T. C. O'KANE,
C. C. McCABE,
JNO. R. SWENEY.

Copyright, 1878, by T. C. O'KANE, C. C. McCABE, and JNO. R. SWENEY.

Joy to the World.

The Lord is Come.

1

WATTS.   Harmonized by T. C. O'K.

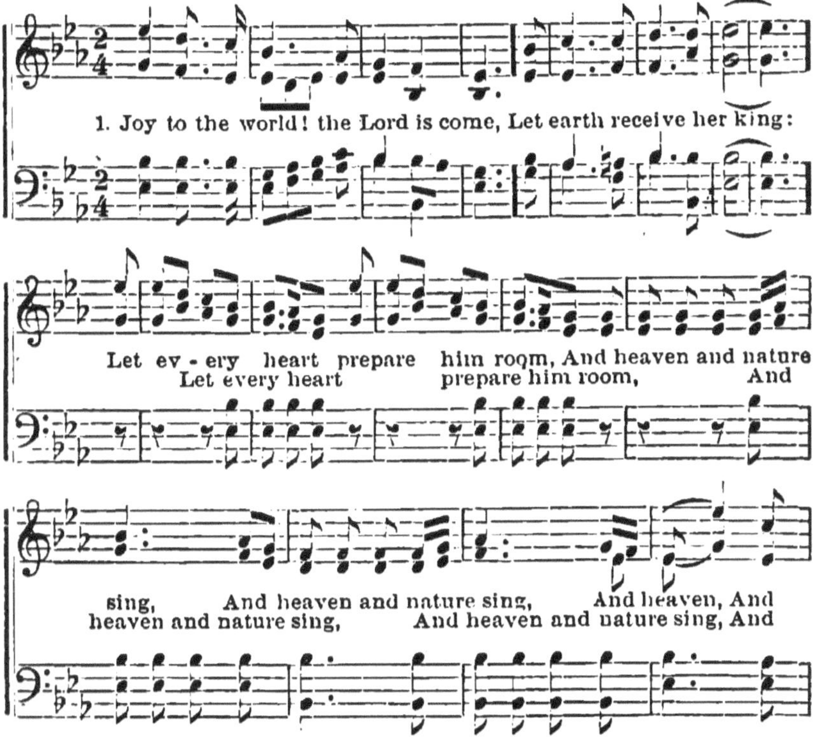

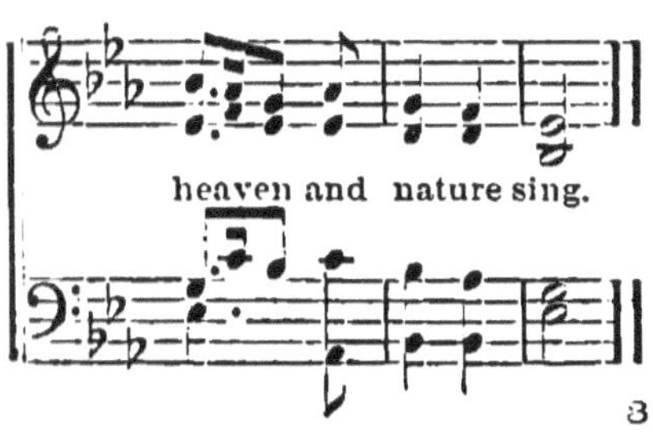

1. Joy to the world! the Lord is come, Let earth receive her king: Let ev-ery heart prepare him room, And heaven and nature sing, And heaven and nature sing, And heaven, And heaven and nature sing.

2. Joy to the world! the Savior reigns;
Let men their songs employ;
While fields and floods, rocks, hills and plains,
Repeat the sounding joy.

3. No more let sin and sorrow grow,
Nor thorns infest the ground:
He comes to make his blessings flow,
Far as the curse is found.

Go to Jesus.

FANNY CROSBY.
JNO. R. SWENEY.

1. Would'st thou find a friend to love thee More than human hearts can love,
2. Would'st thou find the blessed fountain, Flowing at the cross so free?
3. Would'st thou find a friend to teach thee How thy soul by faith may live,
4. Would'st thou find a friend to shield thee, When with clouds thy sky is dim?

One who knows thy every trial? Such a friend thou hast above.
Go to Je-sus; he will guide thee; Cleansed by him thy soul shall be.
How to reach those heights of rapture Earthly joy can never give?
Go to Je-sus; ask his mercy; Lo, he calls thee, go to him.

CHORUS.

Go, in trusting faith believing, Cast thy burden on the Lord,

He has promised to receive thee—Take thy Savior at his word.

Copyrighted 1879, by JNO. R. SWENEY.

To Him be All the Glory.

T. C. O'K. T. C. O'KANE.

1. O let us praise the Savior's name, And tell the wondrous story,
Of him who died for every one, "The Lord of life and glory."
2. To ransom sinners such as we He left his home in heaven,
To save from death a sinful race His precious life was given.
3. This Savior now by faith is mine, My heart with joy is bounding,
And will, throughout eternity, His praises be re-sounding.

CHORUS.

Hal-le-lu-jah! He redeemed us, It is the "old, old story."
Hal-le-lu-jah un-to Je-sus, To him be all the glory.

Copyrighted 1879, by T. C. O'KANE.

5

1 We praise thee, O God! for the Son of thy love,
For Jesus who died, and is now gone above!
CHO.—*Hallelujah! thine the glory, Hallelujah! amen.*
Hallelujah! thine the glory, revive us again.

2 We praise thee, O God! for the Spirit of light,
Who has shown us our Savior, and scattered our night.

3 All glory and praise to the Lamb that was slain,
Who has borne all our sins, and has cleansed every stain.

So I can Wait.

JULIA C. THOMPSON. JOHN R. SWENEY.

1. I know that heav'n lies just beyond This earthly state, this earthly state;
2. I know the heart-aches of this life Will all be healed, will all be healed,
3. I know that when my time shall come To dwell above, to dwell above,

That Christ himself holds death's cold wand; So I can wait, so I can wait.
When the blest peace that ends earth's strife Shall be reveal'd, shall be reveal'd
Jesus his child will welcome home With tend'rest love, with tend'rest love.

I know the dark, mysterious ways My feet may tread, my feet may tread
I know that 'mid the world's turmoil God giveth rest, God giveth rest;
His angel guards will open wide Heav'n's pearly gate, heav'n's pearly gate;

Will all be plain when heav'nly rays Are on them shed, are on them shed.
His arm is round me in its toil; And I am blest, and I am blest.
And I shall then be sat-is-fied: So I can wait, so I can wait!

Copyright, 1878, by JOHN R. SWENEY.

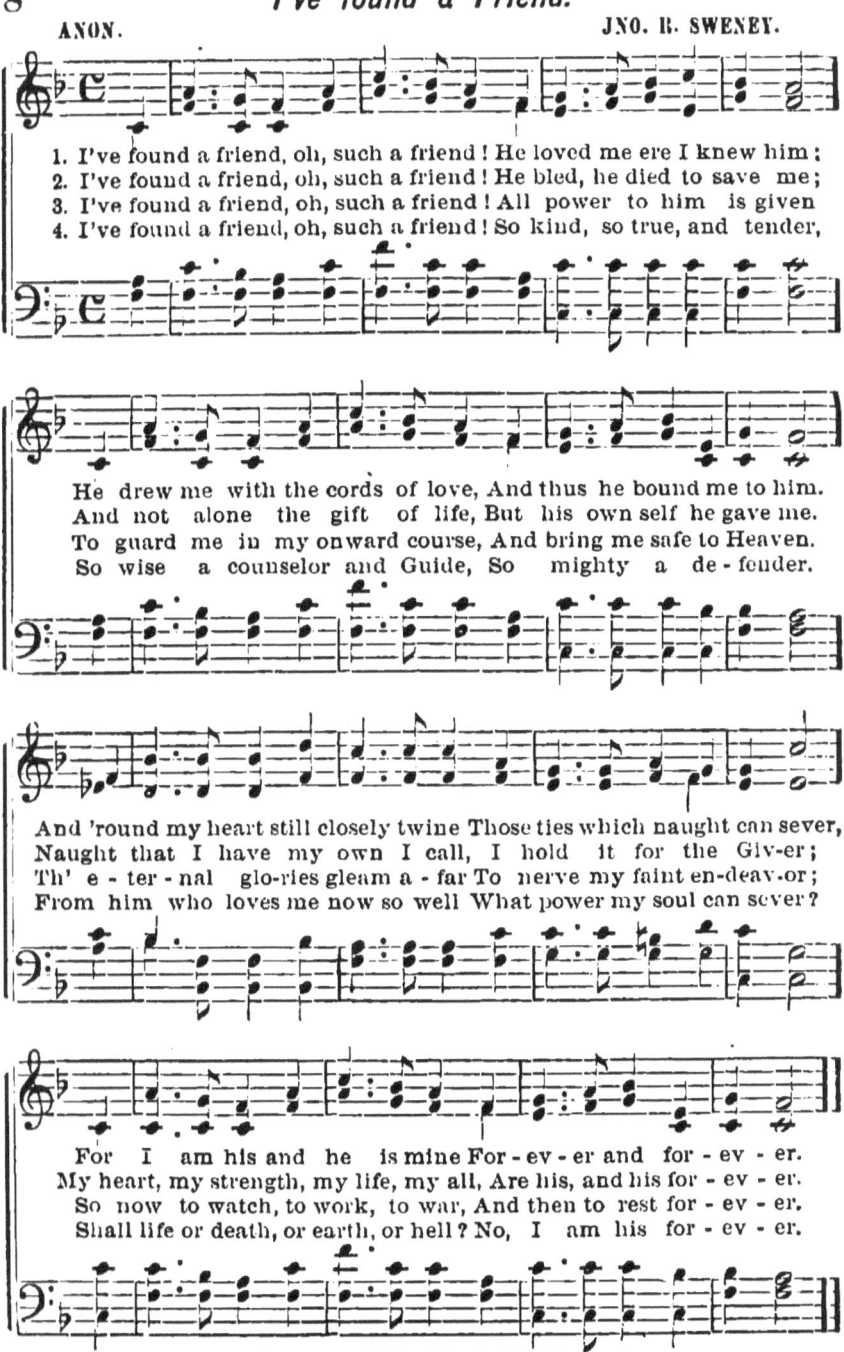

9. As White as Snow.

"Though your sins be as scarlet, they shall be as white as snow."—Isaiah i, 18.

HENRY A. SMITH.   A. O. HUFFMAN.

1. "As white as snow!" Oh can it be, That these sweet words were meant for me.
2. Long time I wandered from my God, In paths by none but sinners trod;
3. He called to me; in vain I sought To turn from him in act or thought;
4. I followed him—he leads me on, The pearly gates are almost won,
5. "As white as snow," was meant for thee, And all who will from sin be free;

Ah, what a rapture 'tis to know, That I may be "as white as snow."
But Jesus sought me there, and oh, His robes were all "as white as snow."
My soul was sick of sin and woe, And longed to be "as white as snow."
Afar the heavenly mansions glow, Where I shall dwell, "as white as snow."
The rich, the poor, the high, the low, Thro' faith may be "as white as snow."

Refrain.

White as snow, white as snow, That I may be as white as snow.

Copyrighted 1879, by T. C. O'KANE.

10.   Praying for You.

1. I have a Savior, he's pleading in glory,
A dear, loving Savior, though earth-friends be few;
And now he is watching in tenderness o'er me,
And oh that my Savior were your Savior too!
CHO.— *For you I am praying, I'm praying for you.*

2. I have a peace: it is calm as a river—
A peace that the friends of this world never knew;
My Savior alone is its Author and Giver,
And oh, could I know it was given to you!

3. When Jesus has found you, tell others the story,
That my loving Savior is your Savior too;
Then pray that your Savior may bring them to glory,
And prayer will be answered — 'twas answered for you!

11. Jesus Will Give You Rest.

FANNY CROSBY.   JNO. R. SWENEY.

1. { Will you come, will you come, with your poor broken heart,
   { Lay it down at the feet of your Savior and Lord,
2. { Will you come, will you come? there is mer-cy for you,
   { On-ly come as you are, and be-lieve on his name
3. { Will you come, will you come? you have nothing to pay;
   { By his death on the cross purchased life for your soul,
4. { Will you come, will you come? how he pleads with you now,
   { And what-ev-er your sin or your sorrow may be,

1st.
Burdened and sin oppressed?
Balm for your aching breast.
Je-sus, who loves you best.
Fly to his lov-ing breast;

2d.
Je-sus will give you rest.
Je-sus, etc.
Je-sus, etc.
Je-sus, etc.

CHORUS.

O happy rest, sweet happy rest, Je-sus will give you rest. happy rest. O, why won't you come in simple, trusting faith?

D. S.

Copyrighted 1879 by JNO. R. SWENEY.

Daily Victory.

From The CHRISTIAN WOMAN.
Moderato.
JNO. R. SWENEY.

1. I want a present living faith, That I may prove each day, each hour,
2. I want a firm, unwavering faith, That bringeth good from seeming ill;
3. I want a faith that falters not, Let skies be bright or tempest beat,

Amid the toils and cares of life, My precious Sa- . . . . . vior's
That, e'en amid affliction's blast, Re - joices in . . . . . . the
That 'mid earth's joys and cares and griefs Victorious sits . . . . . at

love and power, (love and power); I want, a - mid the petty cares That
Father's will, (Father's will); That when long-cherished hope's denied, Still
Je - sus, feet, (Je - sus feet); Give me such faith, and then I know When

daily weary and annoy, To live by faith so near my God
sings a "glad triumphant song," Knowing that he who reigns on high—
I shall pass cold Jordan's wave, The faith that kept me day by day

Copyrighted 1879, by JNO. R. SWENEY.

Oh, How Precious.

T. C. O'K.
T. C. O'KANE.

1. O, how sweet the name of Jesus To believers day by day,
2. O, how sweet the name of Jesus In the time of woe or pain;
3. O, how sweet the name of Jesus In temptation's darkest hour;
4. O, how sweet the name of Jesus Now and evermore will be,

How it thrills the soul with rapture, Toiling up the narrow way.
Peace and comfort always bringing, Bidding joy return again.
In his name we find deliv'rance From the cruel tempter's power.
When the King arrayed in beauty, With the ransomed we shall see.

REFRAIN.

O, how precious, O, how precious Is the dear Redeemer's name;

O, how precious! O, how precious Is the dear Redeemer's name.

Copyright 1875, by T. C. O'KANE.

Leaving All, I follow Thee.

FANNY CROSBY.
Andante.
JNO. R. SWENEY.

1. I will take my cross, and bear it; Thy dis-ci-ple I will be.
2. Lord, thy precious blood has bought me; Thou hast paid the debt for me.
3. O the fullness of thy mercy! O thy wondrous love to me!
4. I will take my cross, and bear it, What-so-e'er that cross may be;

From this moment, blessed Savior, Leaving all, I follow thee.
Now I know the bliss of pardon, Leaving all, I follow thee.
Basking in its glorious sunshine, Leaving all, I follow thee.
For thy sake myself denying, Leaving all, I follow thee.

CHORUS.

Follow thee, through pain and sorrow; Follow where thou leadest me.

From this moment, Blessed Savior, Leaving all, I follow thee.

Copyrighted 1879, by JNO. R. SWENEY.

Evergreen Mountains. Concluded.

faithful and true to the end, He will lead us as upward our
lightful than mortals e'er trod, Where they walk with the saints and the
rapture that never shall cease, Where for-ever flows onward the

footsteps shall tend, To the ever-green mountains of life.
Sav-ior a-broad, Thro' the ever-green mountains of life.
Riv-er of Peace, From the ever-green mountains of life.

Copyrighted 1879, by T. C. O'Kane.

23 Heaven-Whispers.

Gently.   Harmonized by T. C. O'K

[omit in Repeat ..]

[omit in Repeat ..]

1 There's not a bright and beaming smile
Which in the world I see,
But turns my heart to future joy,
And whispers "heaven" to me.
Tho' often here my soul is sad,
And falls the silent tear,
There is a world where all are glad,
And sorrow dwells not there.

2 I never grasp a friendly hand
In greeting or farewell,
But thoughts of an eternal home
Within my bosom swell.
A prayer to meet in heaven at last,
Where all the ransomed come,
And where eternal ages still
Shall find us all at home.

I am the Light.

THEO. HYATT.   *Moderato.*   **JNO. R. SWENEY.**

1. My path is dark, Lord, very dark, No ray of light illumes my way;
A sweet voice whispers, Sad one, hark, [omit 2d time.]
2. I'm burdened, Lord, and sore opprest, I faint beneath the heavy load;
But Jesus says, In me find rest; [omit 2d time.]
3. I'm vile, Lord, very, very vile, And sin assails with mighty power;
A whisper comes, a heavenly smile, [omit 2d time.]
4. I come, dear Lord, with ev'ry cloud,— My burdens all to thee I bring,
And cast my sins, with praises loud, [omit 2d time.]

Oh, hear the blest Redeemer say;
For all along the weary road,
I'll cleanse thy heart this very hour.
On him whose wondrous grace I sing.

LAST CHO. Thou art the light . . . I am the light, I am the light, yes, I am the light,

Thou art the light, I am the light, yes, I am the light . . . . . I am the light.

LAST CHO. Thou art the light, thou art the light, Forever, dear Jesus, I'll
Oh walk in the light, oh
Thou art the light, yes, thou art the light, Forever, dear Jesus, I'll
walk in the light, oh walk in the light, Then visions of bliss will
walk in this light, I'll walk in this light, Lo, visions of bliss now

I am the Light. Concluded.

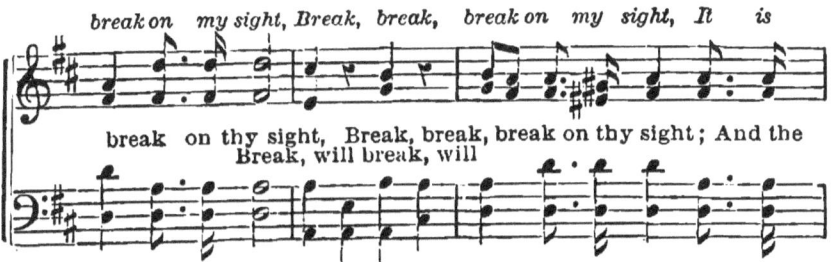

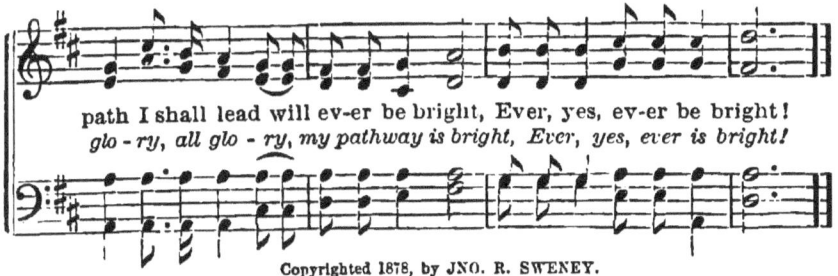

Copyrighted 1878, by JNO. R. SWENEY.

25 Nothing but Leaves.

1 Nothing but leaves! The spirit grieves
O'er years of wasted life;
O'er sins indulged while conscience slept,
O'er vows and promises unkept,
And reap from years of strife—
Nothing but leaves!

2 Nothing but leaves! No gathered sheaves,
Of life's fair ripening grain:
We sow our seeds; lo! tares and weeds,—
Words, idle words, for earnest deeds,-
Then reap, with toil and pain,
Nothing but leaves!

3 Ah, who shall thus the Master meet,
And bring but withered leaves?
Ah, who shall at the Savior's feet,
Before the awful judgment-seat
Lay down for golden sheaves,
Nothing but leaves!

26 Ninety and Nine.

1 There were ninety and nine that safely lay
In the shelter of the fold,
But one was out on the hills away,
Far off from the gates of gold—
Away on the mountains wild and bare,
Away from the tender Shepherd's care.

2 "Lord, thou hast here thy ninety and nine:
Are they not enough for Thee?"
But the Shepherd made answer:
"'T is one of mine
Has wandered away from me:
And although the road be rough and steep
I go to the desert to find my sheep."

3 But none of the ransomed ever knew
How deep were the waters crossed;
Nor how dark was the night that the Lord passed through
Ere he found his sheep that was lost.
Out in the desert he heard its cry—
Sick and helpless, and ready to die.

4 But all through the mountains, thunder-riven,
And up from the rocky steep,
There rose a cry to the gate of heaven
"Rejoice! I have found my sheep!"
And the angels echoed around the throne,
"Rejoice, for the Lord brings back his own!"

27 Beautiful River.

1 Shall we gather at the river
Where bright angel feet have trod
With its crystal tide forever
Flowing by the throne of God?

2 On the margin of the river,
Washing up its silver spray,
We will walk and worship ever
All the happy, golden day.

3 Ere we reach the shining river,
Lay we every burden down;
Grace our spirits will deliver
And provide a robe and crown.

Lost and Saved.

FANNY CROSBY.   JNO. R. SWENEY.

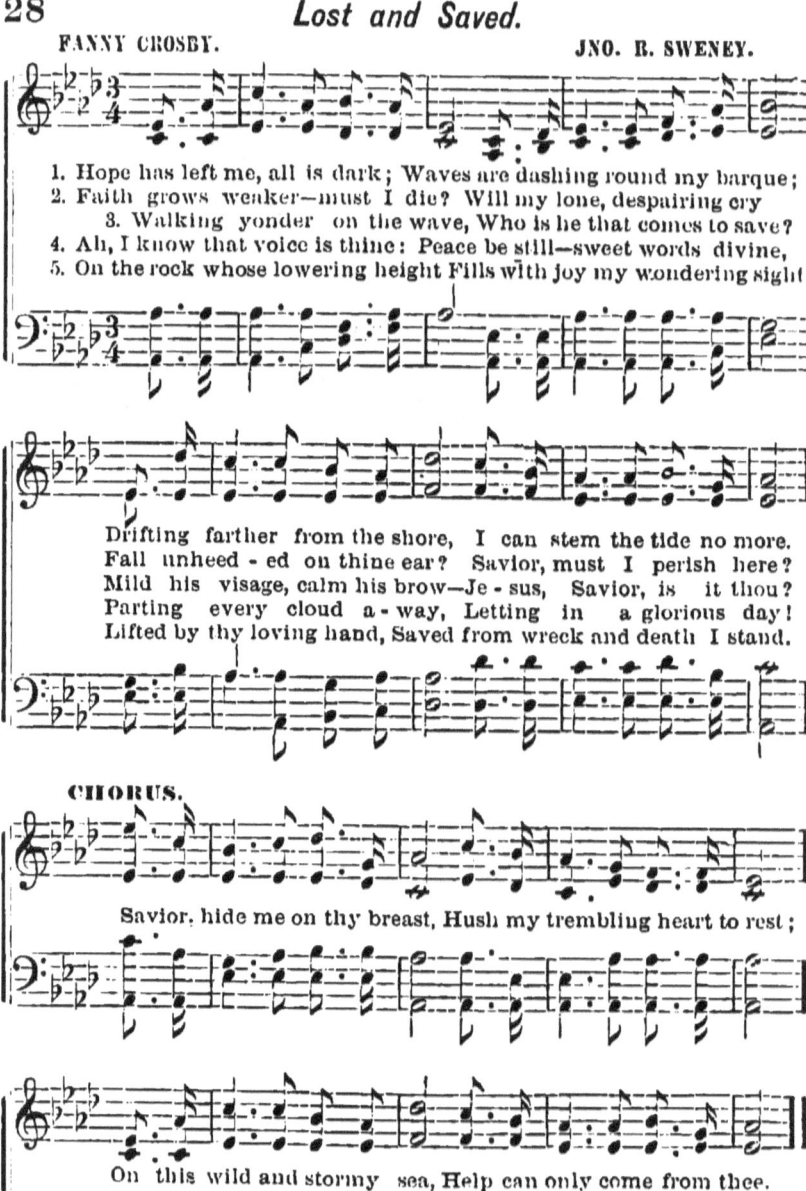

1. Hope has left me, all is dark; Waves are dashing round my barque;
2. Faith grows weaker—must I die? Will my lone, despairing cry
3. Walking yonder on the wave, Who is he that comes to save?
4. Ah, I know that voice is thine: Peace be still—sweet words divine,
5. On the rock whose lowering height Fills with joy my wondering sight,

Drifting farther from the shore, I can stem the tide no more.
Fall unheed - ed on thine ear? Savior, must I perish here?
Mild his visage, calm his brow—Je-sus, Savior, is it thou?
Parting every cloud a-way, Letting in a glorious day!
Lifted by thy loving hand, Saved from wreck and death I stand.

CHORUS.

Savior, hide me on thy breast, Hush my trembling heart to rest;
On this wild and stormy sea, Help can only come from thee.

29. Beautiful Day.

By per. of E. M. BRUCE.   Words and Music by WM. J. KIRKPATRICK.

1. Beautiful day, lovely thy light; Holy each ray, nothing like night!
Cloudless thy sky; peaceful my stay Here in the sunlight of beautiful day.

2. Beautiful day, calm was thy dawn; Joyous the lay, blessed the morn,
When in my heart, over my way, First shone the noontide of beautiful day.

CHORUS.

Beautiful, beautiful day, Evermore shine on my way,
beautiful, beautiful day, Evermore shine on my way,
Savior, I pray, keep me alway, Safe in this beautiful day. Beautiful day.

3 Beautiful day, perfectly bright;
  Jesus alway, boundless delight.
  Bliss all around, heav'n by the way,
  Shining in fullness, oh, beautiful
    day.   CHO.

4 Beautiful day, haven of rest;
  Every one may come and be blest;
  Glory to God, naught can dismay;
  Christ is the light of this beautiful
    day.   CHO.

Satisfied by and by.

Theme of Chorus from WEBSTER.   T. C. O'KANE.

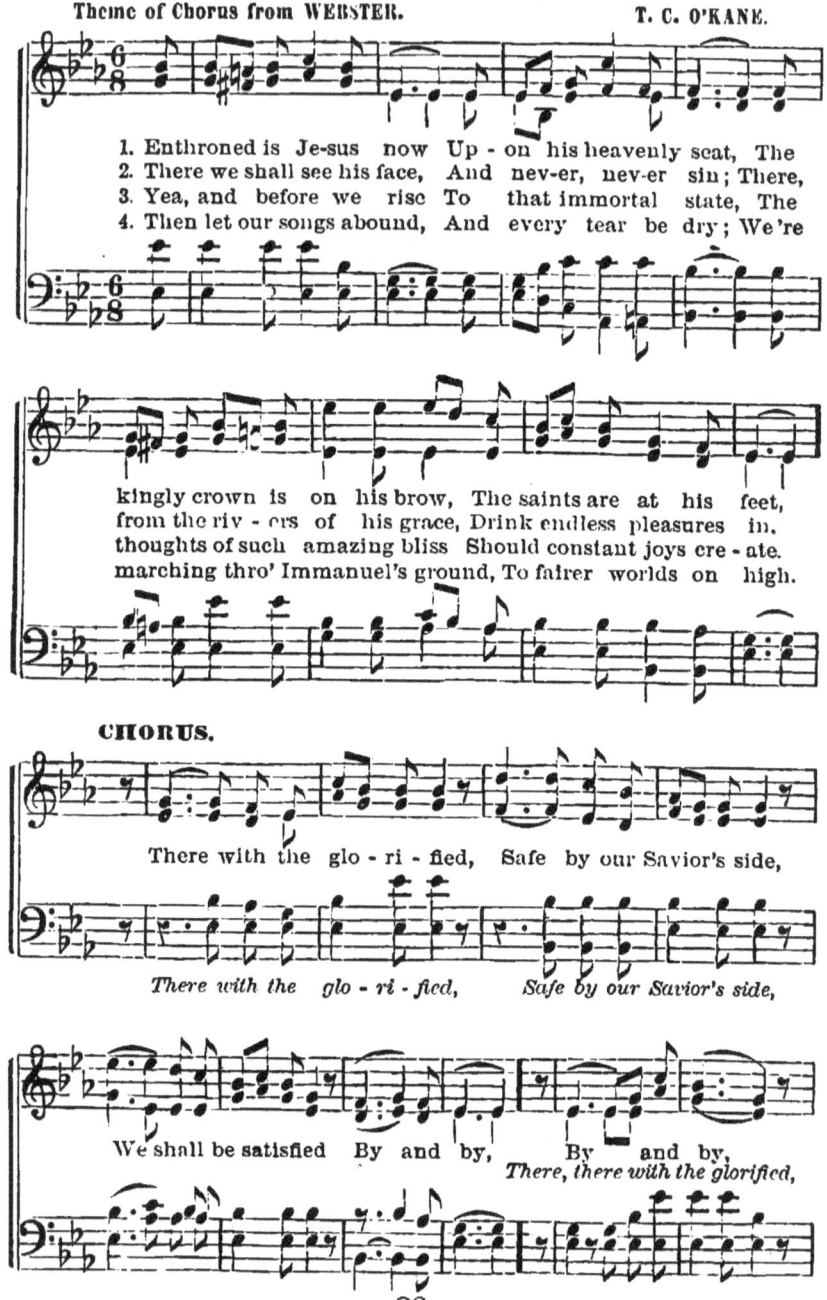

1. Enthroned is Jesus now Upon his heavenly seat, The kingly crown is on his brow, The saints are at his feet,
2. There we shall see his face, And never, never sin; There, from the riv-ers of his grace, Drink endless pleasures in.
3. Yea, and before we rise To that immortal state, The thoughts of such amazing bliss Should constant joys cre-ate.
4. Then let our songs abound, And every tear be dry; We're marching thro' Immanuel's ground, To fairer worlds on high.

CHORUS.

There with the glo-ri-fied, Safe by our Savior's side,
We shall be satisfied By and by, By and by,
There, there with the glorified,

35 The Voice of Jesus.

HORATIUS BONAR, D. D.   T. C. O'KANE.

1. I heard the voice of Je-sus say, "Come unto me and rest.
   Lay down, thou weary one, lay down Thy head upon my breast."
2. I heard the voice of Je-sus say, "Behold I freely give
   The living water, thirsty one, Stoop down and drink and live."
3. I heard the voice of Je-sus say, "I am this dark world's light;
   Look unto me, thy morn shall rise, And all thy day be bright."

I came to Je-sus, as I was, Weary, and worn and sad, I
I came to Je-sus, and I drank Of that life-giv-ing stream, My
I looked to Je-sus, and I found In him my star, my sun, And

found in him a resting place, And he has made me glad.
thirst was quenched, my soul revived, And now I live in him.
in that light of life I'll walk, Till all my journey's done.

36 Beulah.

1 My latest sun is sinking fast,
  My race is nearly run,
My strongest trials now are past,
  My triumph is begun.

CHO. O come, angel band,
     Come and around me stand,
     O bear me away on your snowy
     To my immortal home.   [wings

2 I know I'm nearing the holy ranks
  Of friends and kindred dear,
For I brush the dews on Jordan's
  The crossing must be near.   [banks.

3 O bear my longing heart to him
  Who bled and died for me;
Whose blood now cleanses from all
  And gives me victory.   [sin,

37 Title Clear.

1 When I can read my title clear
  To mansions in the skies,
I'll bid farewell to every fear,
  And wipe my weeping eyes.

CHO. We will stand the storm,
     We will anchor by and by;

2 Should earth against my soul engage,
  And fiery darts be hurl'd,
Then I can smile at Satan's rage,
  And face a frowning world.

3 Let cares like a wild deluge come,
  Let storms of sorrow fall.—
So I but safely reach my home,
  My God, my heaven, my all.

4 There I shall bathe my weary soul
  In seas of heavenly rest,
And not a wave of trouble roll
  Across my peaceful breast.

40. The Standard of the Cross.

T. C. O'KANE.

1. See, on the mountain top The standard of your God! In Jesus' name 'tis lifted up, In Jesus' name 'tis lifted up, All stained with hallowed blood, All stained with hallowed blood.

CHORUS.
Then rally, oh, rally around the standard of the cross,

2 His standard-bearers now
  To all the nations call:
  To Jesus' cross, ye nations, bow;
  He bore the cross for all.

3 Go up with Christ your Head;
  Your Captain's footsteps see;
  Follow your Captain, and be led
  To certain victory.

4 All power to him is given;
  He ever reigns the same:
  Salvation, happiness, and heaven
  Are all in Jesus' name.

5 Strong in the Lord of hosts,
  And in his mighty power,
  Who in the strength of Jesus trusts
  Is more than conqueror.

Copyright, 1878, by T. C. O'KANE.

3 Sinking and panting as for breath
  I knew not help was near me;
  I cried, "Oh, save me, Lord, from death,
  Immortal Jesus, hear me."
  Then quick as tho't I felt him mine,
  My Savior stood before me;
  I saw his brightness round me shine,
  And shouted "GLORY, GLORY."

4 O sacred hour! O hallowed spot!
  Where love divine first found me;
  Wherever falls my distant lot
  My heart shall linger round thee.
  And when from earth I rise, to soar
  Up to my home in heaven,
  Down will I cast my eyes once more,
  Where I was first forgiven.

42. I do Believe the Savior.

EDGAR PAGE.   JNO. R. SWENEY.

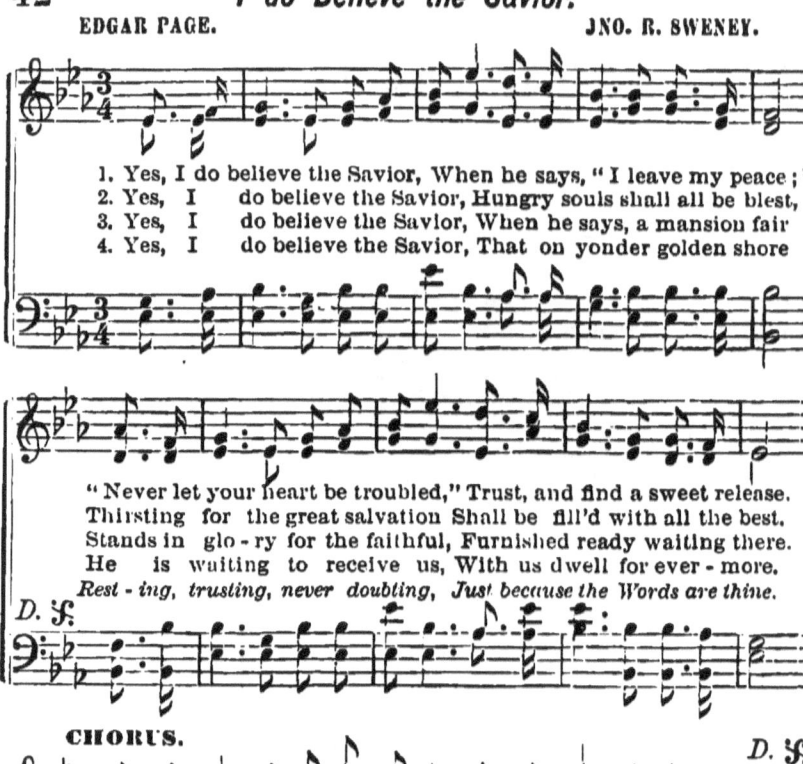

1. Yes, I do believe the Savior, When he says, "I leave my peace;"
2. Yes, I do believe the Savior, Hungry souls shall all be blest,
3. Yes, I do believe the Savior, When he says, a mansion fair
4. Yes, I do believe the Savior, That on yonder golden shore

"Never let your heart be troubled," Trust, and find a sweet release.
Thirsting for the great salvation Shall be fill'd with all the best.
Stands in glo-ry for the faithful, Furnished ready waiting there.
He is waiting to receive us, With us dwell for ever-more.

Rest-ing, trusting, never doubting, Just because the Words are thine.

CHORUS.

Savior, I will take thy promise, Ev'ry precious promise mine;

Copyrighted 1879, by JNO. R. SWENEY.

43. Toiling up the Way.

1 We are toiling up the way,
   Narrow way, narrow way,
We have journeyed many a day,
   Toward the kingdom.
Toward the distant shining land,
   Golden land, golden land,
Where the heavenly harpers stand
   In the kingdom.

CHO.—*Still we sing, Christ our King
   Walks with us the weary way,
And the shining angels wait,
   Angels wait, angels wait,
To unbar the golden gate
   To the kingdom.*

2 Though the journey may be long,
   Hard and long, hard and long,
We will cheer it with a song
   Of the kingdom.
We shall enter by the cross,
   Blessed cross, blessed cross,
Gaining gold that hath no dross,
   In the kingdom.

3 We shall know each other there,
   Over there, over there,
When our angel robes we wear
   In the kingdom.
All that's purest, holiest here, [dear,
   Grows more dear, grows more
In the mansions drawing near,
   In the Kingdom.

46
1 Watchman, tell us of the night,
  What its signs of promise are;
Trav'ler, o'er yon mountain's height,
  See that glory-beaming star.
Watchman, does its beauteous ray
  Aught of hope or joy foretell?
Trav'ler, yes, it brings the day,
  Promised day of Israel.

2 Watchman, tell us of the night;
  Higher yet that star ascends.
Trav'ler, blessedness and light,
  Peace and truth its course portends.
Watchman, will its beams, alone,
  Gild the spot that gave them birth?
Trav'ler, ages are its own;
  See, it bursts o'er all the earth.

3 Watchman, tell us of the night,
  For the morning seems to dawn.
Trav'ler, darkness takes its flight;
  Doubt and terror are withdrawn.
Watchman, let thy wand'ring cease;
  Hie thee to thy quiet home.
Trav'ler, lo! the Prince of Peace,
  Lo! the Son of God is come.

47
1 Rise, my soul, and stretch thy wings;
  Thy better portion trace;
Rise from transitory things,
  Tow'rd heaven, thy native place.
Sun, and moon, and stars decay;
  Time shall soon this earth remove;
Rise, my soul, and haste away
  To seats prepared above.

2 Rivers to the ocean run,
  Nor stay in all their course;
Fire, ascending, seeks the sun;
  Both speed them to their source:
So a soul that's born of God,
  Pants to view his glorious face;
Upward tends to his abode,
  To rest in his embrace.

3 Cease, ye pilgrims, cease to mourn;
  Press onward to the prize;
Soon our Savior will return,
  Triumphant in the skies:
There we'll join the heavenly train,
  Welcomed to partake the bliss;
Fly from sorrow, care, and pain,
  To realms of endless peace.

51. Jesus Only.

"And suddenly, they saw no man any more, save Jesus only with themselves."—MARK ix., 8.

JANE CREWDSON.   LUCY J. RIDER.

1. Je-sus on-ly! Let the vis-ion In its glo-ry pass a-way;
2. When we leave the height of Tabor For earth's valleys, dim and cold,
3. When our path seems dark and lonely, Comforts failing poor and sad,

Van-ish all the light E-lys-ian! 'T is enough if Je-sus stay;
'Mid life's toil and care and labor, On-ly Je-sus can up-hold.
Friends estranged, with Je-sus on-ly We are rich, and full, and glad.

Refrain.

Je-sus on-ly! Je-sus on-ly! Can my inmost soul now say:

Je-sus on-ly! Je-sus on-ly! 'T is enough if Je-sus stay.

The Mercy Seat.

FANNY J. CROSBY. JNO. R. SWENEY.

1. From worldly thought and busy care We come to seek the place of prayer,
2. O hallowed hour that nearer brings To mortal view eternal things,
3. Come, burdened soul, if such there be, Who from thy sorrow would'st be free;
4. Praise God that all the cross may bear, Praise God that all a crown may wear

Where Jesus condescends to meet His children at the mercy seat.
While here we hold communion sweet With Jesus at the mercy seat.
Thy loving Savior now will meet, And cleanse thee at the mercy seat.
Praise God for such an hour so sweet, Of blessing at the mercy seat.

CHORUS.

The mercy seat, the mercy seat, Our only safe and sure retreat;

Though storms without may wildly beat, 'Tis sunshine at the mercy seat.

Copyrighted 1879, by JNO. R. SWENEY.

53. Thy Light is Come.

Rev. H. BONAR, D. D.
T. C. O'KANE.

Spirited.

1. Out of darkness in-to light / Out of midnight in-to day } Jesus calls the sons of night; [omit............]
2. From this world's alluring snares, / From its van-i-ty and strife } From its perils and its cares, [omit............]
3. From the van-ities of youth, / In-to joy that nev-er palls, } Into rest and love and truth, [omit............]

CHORUS.

1. Jesus bids us come away.
2. Jesus beckons us to life.
3. Jesus in his mercy calls.

Arise and shine; Arise and shine; Arise and shine;
Arise and shine, Arise, thy light is come. is come. Arise and shine.
Arise and shine, Arise and shine, Thy glorious light is come.

Copyrighted 1879, by T. C. O'KANE.

54. The Stranger at the Door.

With feeling.   Revelations iii, 20.   T. C. O'KANE.

1. Behold a stranger at the door; He gently knocks—has knocked before; Has waited long, is waiting still, You treat no other friend so ill.
2. O lovely attitude—he stands With melting heart and loaded hands; O matchless, kindness—and he shows This matchless kindness to his foes.
3. But will he prove a friend indeed? He will—the very friend you need. The friend of sinners? Yes, 't is he, With garments dyed on Calvary.
4. Rise, touched with gratitude divine; Turn out his enemy and thine; That soul-destroying monster, sin, And let the heavenly Stranger in.
5. Admit him, ere his anger burn—His feet, departed, ne'er return; Admit him, or the hour 's at hand, You 'll at *his* door rejected stand.

O, let the dear Savior come in, He'll cleanse the heart from sin; O keep him no more, out at the door, But let the dear Savior come in.

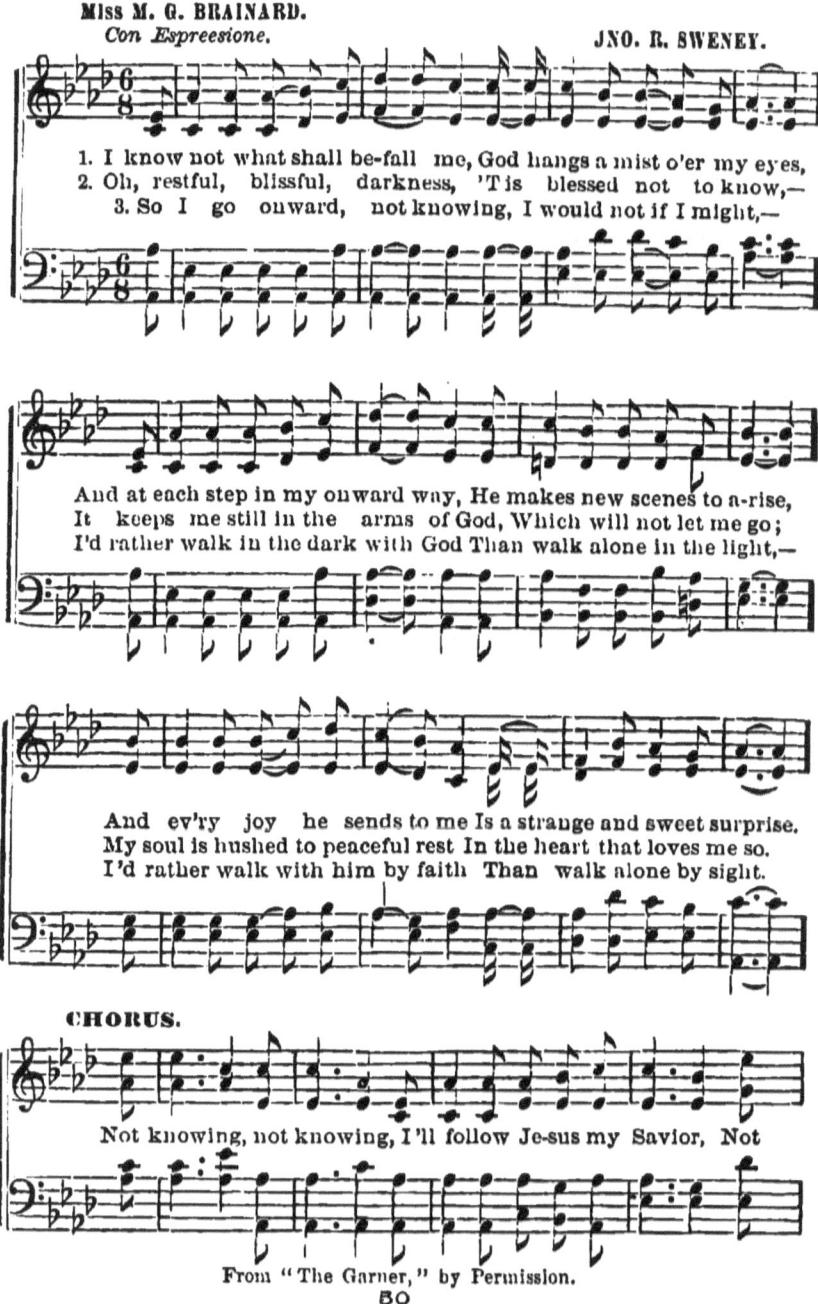

Not Knowing. Concluded.

know-ing, not know-ing, I'll fol-low wher-e'er he leads.

57. Jesus Reigns.

Lively. T. C. O'KANE.

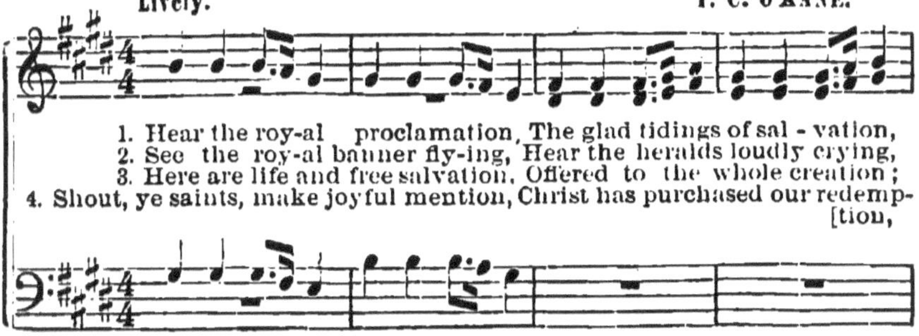

1. Hear the roy-al proclamation, The glad tidings of sal-vation,
2. See the roy-al banner fly-ing, Hear the heralds loudly crying,
3. Here are life and free salvation, Offered to the whole creation;
4. Shout, ye saints, make joyful mention, Christ has purchased our redemp-
[tion,

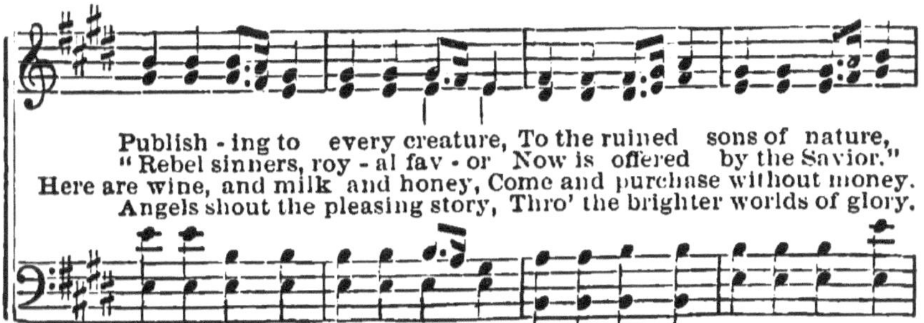

Publish-ing to every creature, To the ruined sons of nature,
"Rebel sinners, roy-al fav-or Now is offered by the Savior."
Here are wine, and milk and honey, Come and purchase without money.
Angels shout the pleasing story, Thro' the brighter worlds of glory.

CHORUS.

Je-sus reigns!
Je-sus reigns! { Lo! he reigns, he reigns victorious } Je-sus reigns!
Je-sus reigns! { Over heaven and earth most glorious. }
Je-sus reigns!

Weary Not. Concluded.

way, / Weary by the way, What ever by thy lot; be thy lot; There awaits a brighter day, / day, a brighter day, To all, to all who weary not, weary not.

65. No Crumb for Me?

Rev. Wm. P. BREED.   J. E. GOULD.

1. { Passing, Lord, by vale and mountain, Highway, byway, thro' the land, / Bringing wine from Calv'ry's fountain, Bread from God's free-giving hand.
2. { On, dear Lord, pursue thy mission To the lost of Is-ra-el: / Yet, give ear to my pe-tition, Pit-y-ing Im-man-u-el!
3. { Wretched, wayworn, grief-o'ertaken, Low at thy kind feet I bow, / Hun-gry, naked, blind, for-saken, Je-sus, feed me—feed me now!

Cho. Feed me now, feed me now, Je-sus feed me—feed me now.

CHORUS.

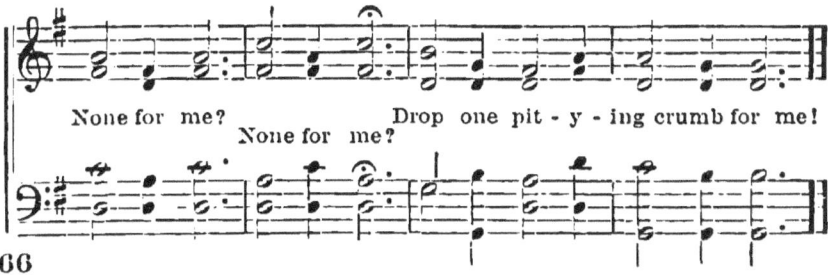

None for me? / None for me? Drop one pit-y-ing crumb for me!

66

1 Lord I hear of showers of blessings
Thou art scatt'ring full and free.
Showers the thirsty land refreshing,
Let some droppings fall on me.
    Even me.

2 Pass me not; thy lost one bringing,
Bind my heart, O Lord, to thee;
While the streams of love are
[springing,
Blessing others, O bless me. *Even me.*

67. Song Memories.

S. J. V. (Mear for Introduction.) S. J. VAIL.

Why do we mourn departing friends, Or shake at death's alarms?

'Tis but the voice that Je-sus sends, To call them to his arms.

1. What mem'ries are stirred within me, Recalled by that hymn so dear,
2. I think of my early childhood, So blest by her tender care,
3. The depth of my soul's affection, Alas, I could nev-er tell,
4. No wonder my eyes are weeping Such bitter and lonely tears,

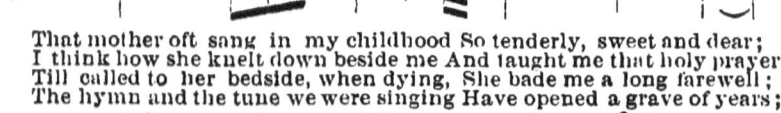

That mother oft sang in my childhood So tenderly, sweet and dear;
I think how she knelt down beside me And taught me that holy prayer:
Till called to her bedside, when dying, She bade me a long farewell;
The hymn and the tune we were singing Have opened a grave of years;

68. Beyond the River.

1 We shall meet beyond the river,
  By and by, by and by;
And the darkness shall be over,
  By and by, by and by;
With the toilsome journey don
And the glorious battle won,
We shall shine forth as the sun,
  By and by, by and by.

2 There our tears shall all cease flow-
  By and by, by and by; [ing,
And with sweetest rapture knowing,
  By and by, by and by.
All the blest ones who have gone
To the land of life and song,—
We with shoutings shall rejoin,
  By and by, by and by.

69. Encouragements to Pray.

1 Come, my soul, thy suit prepare;
Jesus loves to answer prayer;
He himself invites thee near,
Bids thee ask him, waits to hear.

2 Lord, I come to thee for rest;
Take possession of my breast;
There thy blood-bought right main-
And without a rival reign. [tain,

3 While I am a pilgrim here,
Let thy love my spirit cheer;
As my guide, my guard, my friend,
Lead me to my journey's end.

4 Show me what I have to do;
Every hour my strength renew;
Let me live a life of faith,—
Let me die thy people's death.

The New Song. Concluded.

ran - som'd throng: .. Pow-er and do-min-ion to him that shall
ransom'd, the ransom'd throng: ..

reign; Glo-ry and praise to the Lamb that was slain.
that shall reign;

Lamb of Calvary.

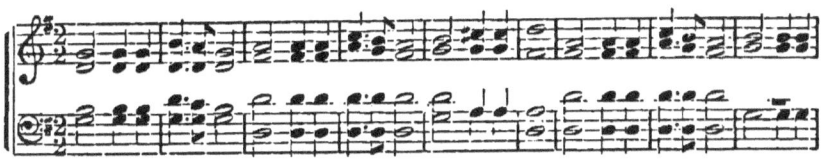

73   **Before the Cross.**
1 My faith looks up to thee,
Thou Lamb of Calvary:
  Savior divine,
Now hear me while I pray;
Take all my guilt away;
  O let me, from this day,
    Be wholly thine.

2 May thy rich grace impart
Strength to my fainting heart;
  My zeal inspire;
As thou hast died for me,
O may my love to thee
Pure, warm, and changeless be—
  A living fire.

3 While life's dark maze I tread,
And griefs around me spread,
  Be thou my Guide;
Bid darkness turn to day;
Wipe sorrow's tears away,
Nor let me ever stray
  From thee aside.

4 When ends life's transient dream;
When death's cold, sullen stream
  Shall o'er me roll;
Blest Savior, then in love,
Fear and distress remove;
O, bear me safe above,—
  A ransom'd soul.

74   **Invocation.**
1 Come, thou Almighty King,
Help us thy Name to sing,
  Help us to praise;
Father all glorious,
O'er all victorious,
Come and reign over us,
  Ancient of days.

2 Come, thou Incarnate Word,
Gird on thy mighty sword,
  Our prayer attend;
Come and thy people bless,
And give thy word success;
Spirit of holiness,
  On us descend.

3 Come, Holy Comforter,
Thy sacred witness bear
  In this glad hour;
Thou who Almighty art,
Now rule in every heart,
And ne'er from us depart,
  Spirit of power.

As Pants the Hart. Concluded.

streams, So pants my soul, O Lord, for thee.
for cooling streams, So pants my soul,

76   He Leadeth Me.

1 He leadeth me! oh, blessed thought!
Oh, words with heavenly comfort fraught!
Whate'er I do, where'er I be,
Still 'tis God's hand that leadeth me.

REF.—*He leadeth me! he leadeth me!*
By his own hand he leadeth me!
His faithful foll'wer I would be,
For by his hand he leadeth me.

2 Lord, I would clasp thy hand in mine,
Nor ever murmur nor repine—
Content, whatever lot I see,
Since 'tis my God that leadeth me.

3 And when my task on earth is done,
When, by thy grace the victory's won,
E'en death's cold wave I will not flee,
Since God thro' Jordan leadeth me.

77   What Shall the Harvest Be?*

1 Sowing the seed by the daylight fair,
Sowing the seed by the noonday glare,
Sowing the seed by the fading light,
Sowing the seed in the solemn night;
Oh, what shall the harvest be?

CHORUS.

Sown in the darkness or sown in the light,
Sown in our weakness or sown in our might,
Gathered in time or eternity,
Sure, ah, sure will the harvest be.

2 Sowing the seed by the wayside high,
Sowing the seed on the rocks to die,
Sowing the seed where the thorns will spoil,
Sowing the seed on the fertile soil;
Oh, what shall the harvest be?

3 Sowing the seed with an aching heart,
Sowing the seed while the tear-drops start,
Sowing in hope till the reapers come,
Gladly to gather the harvest home;
Oh, what shall the harvest be?

78   Sweet Hour of Prayer.

1 Sweet hour of prayer,
  Sweet hour of prayer!
That calls me from a world of care,
And bids me at my Father's throne
Make all my wants and wishes known;

* Bliss's music, owned by S. Brainards' Sons.

In seasons of distress or grief,
My soul has often found relief,
And oft escaped the tempter's snare,
By thy return, sweet hour of prayer.

2 Sweet hour of prayer,
  Sweet hour of prayer!
Thy wings shall my petition bear,
To him whose truth and faithfulness
Engage the waiting soul to bless;
And since he bids me seek his face,
Believe his word and trust his grace,
I'll cast on him my every care,
And wait for thee, sweet hour of pray'r.

79   To-day.

1 To-day the Savior calls;
  Ye wanderers, come;
Oh, ye benighted souls,
  Why longer roam?

2 To-day the Savior calls;
  Oh, listen now;
Within these sacred walls
  To Jesus bow.

3 The Spirit calls to-day;
  Yield to his power;
Oh, grieve him not away;
  'Tis mercy's hour.

80   What For Me?

1 I gave my life for thee,
  My precious blood I shed,
That thou might'st ransomed be,
  And quickened from the dead;
I gave, I gave my life for thee,
What hast thou given for me?

2 My Father's house of light—
  My glory-circled throne,
I left, for earthly night,
  For wanderings sad and lone:
I left, I left it all for thee:
Hast thou left aught for me?

3 And I have brought to thee,
  Down from my home above,
Salvation full and free,
  My pardon and my love;
I bring, I bring rich gifts to thee,
What hast thou brought to me?

One Step More. Concluded.

82 For Me.
S. J. VAIL.

1 ALAS! and did my Savior bleed?
  And did my Sov'reign die?
  Would he devote that sacred head
  For such a worm as I?
CHO. *Jesus died for you,*
   Jesus died for me,
   Yes, Jesus died for all mankind,
   Bless God, salvation's free.

2 Was it for crimes that I have done,
  He groan'd upon the tree?
  Amazing pity! grace unknown!
  And love beyond degree!

3 Well might the sun in darkness hide,
  And shut his glories in,
  When Christ, the mighty Maker, died,
  For man, the creature's sin.

4 Thus might I hide my blushing face
  While his dear cross appears;
  Dissolve my heart in thankfulness,
  And melt mine eyes to tears.

5 But drops of grief can ne'er repay
  The debt of love I owe:
  Here, Lord, I give myself away,—
  'Tis all that I can do.

There's a Land far Away.

Words by J. G. CLARK. Harmonized by T. C. O'K.

1. There's a land far away 'mid the stars we are told, Where they know not the sorrows of time.
 Where the pure waters flow, thro' the valleys of gold, And where life is a treasure sublime.
D. C. Where the way-weary traveler reaches his goal, On the ev-er-green mountains of life.

'Tis the land of our God—'tis the home of the soul, Where the ages of splendor e-ternally roll.

By Permission of O. Ditson & Co.

2 Here our gaze can not soar to that beautiful land,
  But our visions have told of its bliss;
And our souls by the gale from its gardens are fanned,
  When we faint in the deserts of this.
And we sometimes have longed for its holy repose
  When our hearts have been rent with temptations and woes,
And we've drank from the tide of the river that flows
  From the ever-green mountains of life.

3 Oh the stars never tread the blue heavens at night,
  But we think where the ransomed have trod;
And the day never smiles from his palace of light,
  But we feel the bright smile of our God.
We are traveling home thro' earth's changes and gloom,
  To a region where pleasures unchangingly bloom,
And our guide is the glory that shines thro' the tomb,
  From the ever-green mountains of life.

The Rock that is Higher.

E. JOHNSON.   W. G. FISCHER, by Per.

1 Oh, sometimes the shadows are deep,
And rough seems the path to the goal,
And sorrows, how often they sweep
Like tempests down over the soul.
Cho.

2 Oh, sometimes how long seems the day,
And sometimes how heavy my feet;
But toiling in life's dusty way,
The Rock's blessed shadow, how sweet!
Cho.

3 Oh, near to the Rock let me keep,
Or blessings, or sorrows prevail;
Or climbing the mountain way steep,
Or walking the shadowy vale.
Cho.—Then quick, &c.

While the Years are Rolling On. Concluded.

86. The Great Gift.

1 All glory and praise to Jesus our Lord,
So plenteous in grace, and so true to his word.
Cho.—*Hallelujah, thine the glory! hallelujah, amen!*
Hallelujah, thine the glory! revive us again.

2 To us he hath given the gift from above—
The earnest of heaven, the Spirit of love.—*Cho.*

3 Ye all may receive, on Jesus who call,
The gift of his Spirit, 'tis proffered to all.—*Cho.*

4 The peace and the power, ye sinners, embrace,
And look for the shower—the Spirit of grace.—*Cho.*

5 The Giver and gift we all may receive,
Forever and ever within us to live.—*Cho.*

87. How Firm a Foundation.

1 How firm a foundation, ye saints of the Lord,
Is laid for your faith in his excellent word!
What more can he say than to you he hath said,
You who unto Jesus for refuge have fled?
Cho.—*Oh, sing of his mighty love, sing of his mighty love,*
Sing of his mighty love, mighty to save.

2 Fear not, I am with thee; oh, be not dismayed;
I, I am thy God, and will still give thee aid;
I'll strengthen thee, help thee, and cause thee to stand,
Upheld by my righteous, omnipotent hand.—*Cho.*

3 The soul that on Jesus hath leaned for repose,
I will not, I will not desert to his foes;
That soul, tho' all hell should endeavor to shake,
I'll never, no, never, no, never forsake.—*Cho.*

4 When thro' fiery trials thy pathway shall lie,
My grace, all-sufficient, shall be thy supply:
The flame shall not hurt thee; I only design
Thy dross to consume, and thy gold to refine.—*Cho.*

89. Linger no Longer.

T. C. O'K.
Theme from T. E. PERKINS.

Ever Flowing. Concluded.

CHORUS.

Ev-er flow- - - -ing, sweetly flow- - - -ing; Precious
Ev-er, ev-er flow-ing, sweetly, sweetly flowing,

fountain, ev-er flowing full and free. Ev-er flow- -ing, sweetly
full and free. Ever, ever flowing,

flow- - - -ing; Precious fountain, ev-er flow-ing, Yes, for me.
Sweetly, sweetly flowing.

91 Silent Night.

1 Silent night! hallowed night!
Land and deep silent sleep,
Softly glitters bright Bethlehem's star,
Beckoning Israel's eye from afar,
| Where the Savior is born. |

2 Silent night! hallowed night!
On the plain wakes the strain.
Sung by heavenly harbingers bright,
Filled with tidings of boundless [delight.
| Jesus, the Savior, has come. |

3 Silent night! hallowed night!
Earth, awake! silence break!
High your chorus of melody raise,
Sing to heaven in anthems of praise,
| Peace forever shall reign. |

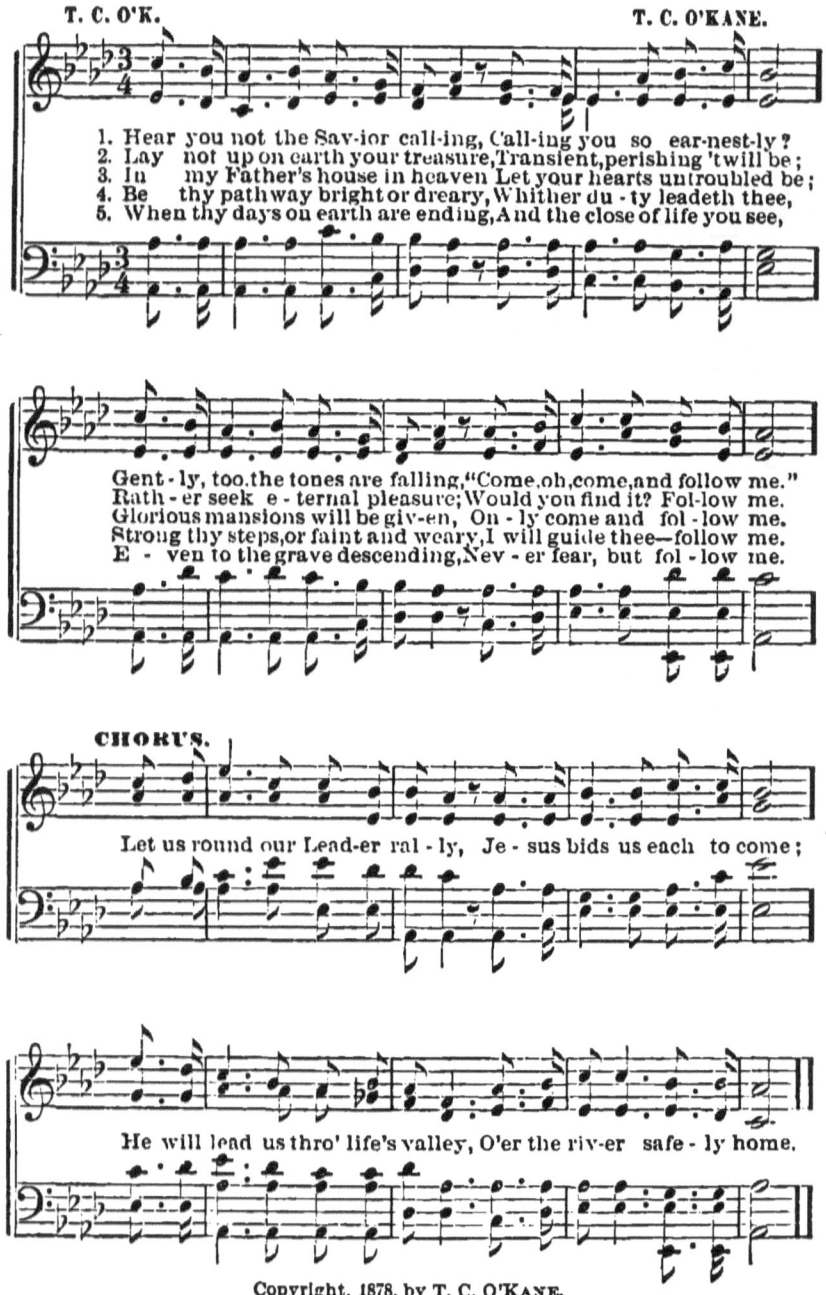

93 MONTGOMERY. Kynett. JNO. R. SWENEY.

1. God shall charge his an-gel le-gions Watch and ward o'er thee to keep;
2. Since with pure and firm af-fec-tion Thou on God hast set thy love,

Tho' thou walk thro' hos-tile re-gions, Tho' in desert wilds thou sleep;
With the wings of his pro-tec-tion He will shield thee from a-bove;

On the li-on vain-ly roar-ing, On his young thy foot shall tread,
Thou shalt call on him in trou-ble, He will heark-en, he will save;

And the drag on's den exploring, Thou shalt bruise the serpent's head.
Here for grief re-ward thee double, Crown with life beyond the grave.

* Small notes may be sung by Soprano, omitting Tenor.

94 **Glorious Things.**

1 Glorious things of thee are spoken,
Zion, city of our God ;
He, whose word can not be broken,
Formed thee for his own abode ;
On the Rock of ages founded,
What can shake thy sure repose ?
With salvation's wall surrounded,
Thou may'st smile at all thy foes.

2 Round each habitation hovering,
See the cloud and fire appear!
For a glory and a covering,
Showing that the Lord is near:
He who gives us daily manna,
He who listens when we cry,
Let him hear the loud hosanna
Rising to his throne on high.

Copyright, 1878, by JOHN R. SWENEY.

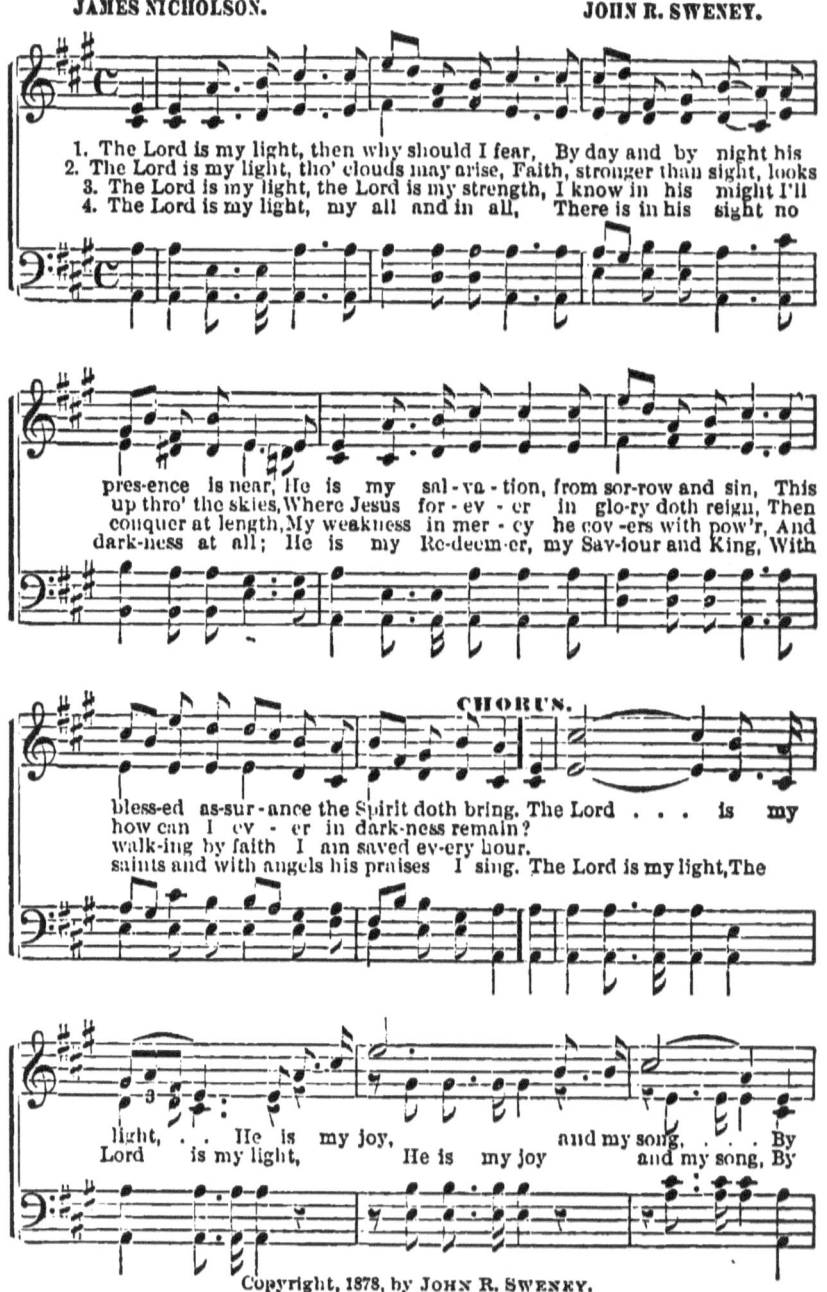

The Lord is my Light. Concluded.

day . . . and by night.
day and by night, by day and by night, He leads, he leads me along.

96 I Love to Tell the Story.

1 I love to tell the story
  Of unseen things above,
  Of Jesus and his glory,
  Of Jesus and his love.
  I love to tell the story,
  Because I know 'tis true;
  It satisfies my longings,
  As nothing else can do.

CHORUS:
*I love to tell the story,
'Twill be my theme in glory
To tell the old, old story
Of Jesus and his love.*

2 I love to tell the story:
  More wonderful it seems
  Than all the golden fancies
  Of all our golden dreams.
  I love to tell the story,
  It did so much for me,
  And that is just the reason
  I tell it now to thee.—*Cho.*

3 I love to tell the story;
  For those who know it best
  Seem hungering and thirsting
  To hear it like the rest.
  And when, in scenes of glory,
  I sing the NEW, NEW SONG,
  'Twill be the OLD, OLD STORY
  That I have loved so long.—*Cho.*

97 Keep on Praying.

1 Long my spirit pined in sorrow,
  Watching, waiting all in vain;
  Waiting for the golden morrow,
  Free from worldly care and pain.
  When I heard a sweet voice saying,
  In the accents of a friend,
  Cheer up, brother; "Keep on praying,"
  Keep on praying to the end.

2 Ye who sigh for holy pleasures,
  Ye who mourn your load of sin,
  "Keep on praying;" heav'nly treasures
  In the end you're sure to win.
  Wrestle with the Lord of glory,
  Lay your treasures at his feet;
  Plead with faith in Calvary's story,
  Till your joys are all complete.

98 What a Friend.

1 What a friend we have in Jesus,
  All our sins and griefs to bear;
  What a privilege to carry
  Every thing to God in prayer.
  Oh, what peace we often forfeit!
  Oh, what needless pain we bear!
  All because we do not carry
  Every thing to God in prayer.

2 Have we trials and temptations?
  Is there trouble anywhere?
  We should never be discouraged;
  Take it to the Lord in prayer.
  Can we find a Friend so faithful,
  Who will all our sorrows share!
  Jesus knows our every weakness;
  Take it to the Lord in prayer.

3 Are we weak and heavy laden,
  Cumbered with a load of care?
  Precious Savior, still our refuge,
  Take it to the Lord in prayer.
  Do thy friends despise, forsake thee?
  Take it to the Lord in prayer;
  In his arms he'll take and shield thee;
  Thou wilt find a solace there.

99 Jesus Loves Even Me.

1 Jesus loves me, and I know I love him,
  It was love brought him my soul to redeem;
  Yes it was love made him die on the tree,
  Oh, I am certain that Jesus loves me.

CHORUS:
*I am so glad that Jesus loves me,
Jesus loves even me.*

2 In this assurance I find sweetest rest;
  Trusting in Jesus I know I am blest;
  Satan dismayed, from my soul now doth flee,
  When I just tell him that Jesus loves me.

3 Oh, if there's only one song I can sing,
  When in his beauty I see the great King:
  This shall my song in eternity be,
  Oh, what a wonder that Jesus loves me.

100. "It is Good to be Here."

Rev. ISAAC N. WILSON.   *JNO. R. SWENEY.*

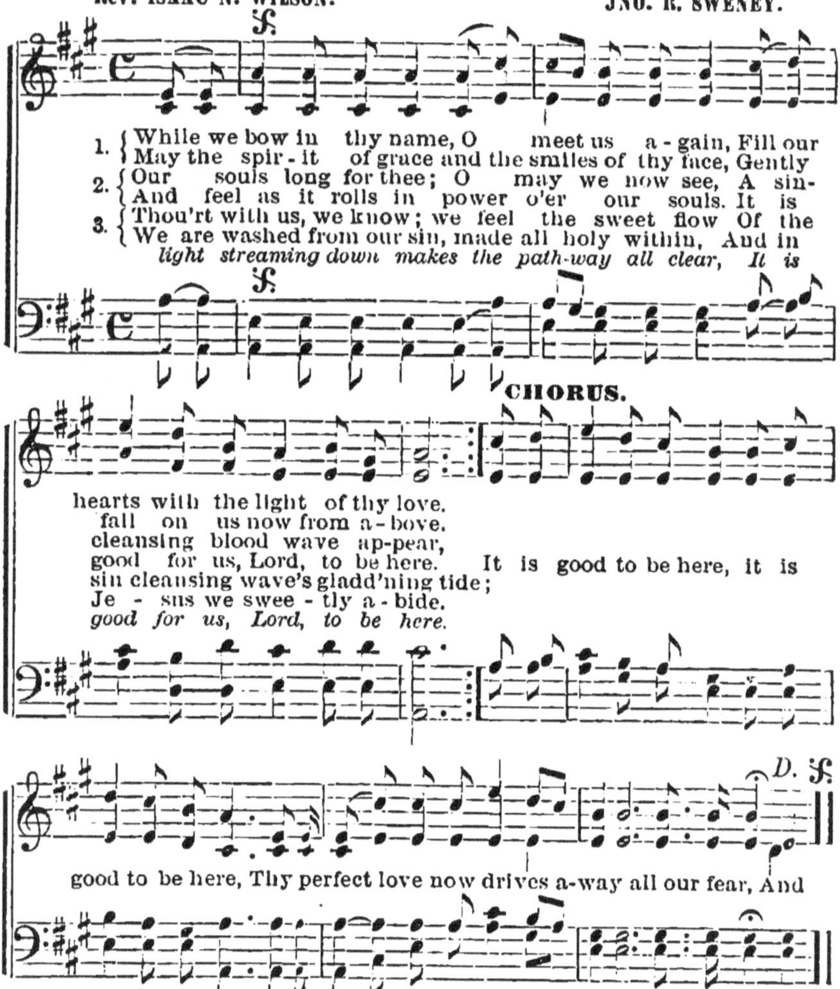

1. While we bow in thy name, O meet us a-gain, Fill our hearts with the light of thy love.
   May the spir-it of grace and the smiles of thy face, Gently fall on us now from a-bove.
2. Our souls long for thee; O may we now see, A sin-cleansing blood wave ap-pear,
   And feel as it rolls in power o'er our souls. It is good for us, Lord, to be here.
3. Thou'rt with us, we know; we feel the sweet flow Of the sin cleansing wave's gladd'ning tide;
   We are washed from our sin, made all holy within, And in Je-sus we swee-tly a-bide.

light streaming down makes the path-way all clear,   *good for us, Lord, to be here.*

CHORUS.

It is good to be here, it is good to be here, Thy perfect love now drives a-way all our fear, And

Copyrighted 1879, by JNO. R. SWENEY.

101. The Convert.—*Tune on opposite page.*

1. O how happy are they
Who the Savior obey,
And have laid up their treasures above;
Tongue can never express
The sweet comfort and peace
Of a soul in its earliest love.

2. That sweet comfort was mine,
When the favor divine
I received through the blood of the Lamb;
When my heart first believed,
What a joy I received—
What a heaven in Jesus' name?

3. 'T was a heaven below
My Reedemer to know,
And the angels could do nothing more
Than to fall at his feet,
And the story repeat,
And the Lover of sinners adore.

4. Jesus, all the day long,
Was my joy and my song:
O that all his salvation might see;
He hath loved me, I cried.
He hath suffer'd and died,
To redeem even rebels like me.

This may be sung also to the tune on this page, by using double stanzas.

102. The Beloved.

JOSEPH SWAIN.   Harmonized by T. C. O'K.

1. O thou, in whose presence my soul takes delight,
On whom in affliction I call,
My comfort by day and my song in the night,
My hope, my salvation, my all!

2. Where dost thou, dear Shepherd, resort with thy sheep,
To feed them in pastures of love?
Say why in the valley of death should I weep,
Or alone in the wilderness rove?

3. O why should I wander an alien from thee,
Or cry in the desert for bread?
Thy foes will rejoice when my sorrows they see,
And smile at the tears I have shed.

4. Ye daughters of Zion, declare, have you seen
The star that on Israel shone?
Say, if in your tents my Beloved has been,
And where with his flocks he is gone.

5. He looks! and ten thousands of angels rejoice,
And myriads wait for his word:
He speaks! and eternity filled with his voice
Re-echoes the praise of the Lord.

6. Dear Shepherd! I hear and will follow thy call:
I know the sweet sound of thy voice;
Restore and defend me, for thou art my all,
And in thee I'll ever rejoice.

103. I need Thee Now.

1. I need thy presence, Lord,
In every hour,
To be my constant shield
From Satan's power.

CHO.—*I need thee, dearest Savior,
Even now I need thee;
O ever grant this favor,
"Abide with me."*

2. I need thy guidance, Lord,
Through every day,
To guide my feet along
Life's devious way.

3. I need thy spirit, Lord,
Yes, all the time,
To show in word and deed
That I am thine.

4. I need thy pardon, Lord;
Bestow it now,
While at the mercy seat
I humbly bow.

104. Only in the Cross.

1. On the cross the Savior's blood
Flowed for our salvation,
Streaming forth, a healing tide,
Unto every nation.

CHO.—*"God forbid! God forbid
I should ever glory
Saving in the cross of Christ,"—
Cross of sacred story.*

2. On the cross the Savior paid
All that I was owing,
Thanks for such a priceless gift
In my heart are glowing.

3. On the cross the Savior spoke
Many sins forgiven,
Then the pardoned sinner bore
With him into heaven.

4. Precious Savior, blessed cross!
Always keep before me;
All along the path of life,
Throw thy shadow o'er me.

106. Jesus' Blood.

FANNY CROSBY. — JNO. R. SWENEY.

1. The blood of Jesus' precious gift, More dear than aught beside;
The blood within the sacred fount, That opened when he died.
2. The blood of Je-sus, this alone, Can cleanse the soul from sin
Can wash a-way its darkest stain, And make it white and clean.
3. The blood of Je-sus glorious theme, Proclaim it o'er and o'er;
The blood of Jesus saves us now, And saves us ev-er-more.

CHORUS.
The blood of Jesus, praise his name, 'Tis, flowing, flowing still;
O come, and prove its healing power, Come whosoev-er will.

Copyrighted 1879, by JNO. R. SWENEY.

107. The Home of the Soul.

1 I will sing you a song of that beau-
tiful land,
The far away home of the soul,
Where no storms ever beat on the
glittering strand,
While the years of eternity roll.

2 O that home of the soul, in my vis-
ions and dreams
Its bright jasper walls I can see,
Till I fancy but thinly the veil inter-
venes,
Between the fair city and me.

3 That unchangeable home is for you
and for me,
Where Jesus of Nazareth stands;
The King of all kingdoms forever is he,
And he holdeth our crowns in his
hands.

4 O how sweet it will be in that beau-
tiful land,
So free from all sorrow and pain!
With songs on our lips, and with
harps in our hands,
To meet one another again.

108. We're Marching to Zion.*

Spirited.   R. LOWRY.

1. Come, ye that love the Lord, And let your joys be known, Join in a song with sweet accord, Join in a song with sweet accord, While ye surround the throne, While ye surround the throne, While ye sur-
2. Let those refuse to sing Who never knew our God; But servants of the heav'nly King, But servants of the heav'nly King, May speak their joys abroad, May
3. The hill of Zion yields A thousand sacred sweets, Before we reach the heav'nly fields, Before we reach the heav'nly fields, Or walk the golden streets, Or
4. Then let our songs abound, And every tear be dry; We're marching thro' Immanuel's ground, We're marching thro' Immanuel's ground, To fairer worlds on high, To

CHORUS.

ye surround the throne. We're marching to Zion, Beautiful, beautiful
speak their joys abroad. We're marching to Zion, &c.
walk the golden streets. We're marching to Zion, &c.
fairer worlds on high. We're marching to Zion, &c.

round the throne. We're marching on to Zion, Zion, We're marching upward to Zion, The beautiful city of God.
Zion, Zion,

* By permission of BIGLOW & MAIN.

109. Hallelujah, I'll Sing.

JER. INGALLS.   T. C. O'KANE.

1. Oh, who is like Jesus, he's Salem's bright King, He smiles and he loves me and helps me to sing.
2. I'll praise him, I'll praise him and bow to his will, While rivers of pleasure my spirit shall fill.
3. In Jesus, my Saviour, I'm perfectly blest, My life, my salvation, my joy and my rest.
4. His name be my theme and his love be my song, His grace shall inspire both my heart and my tongue.
5. I'm happy, I'm happy, oh, wondrous account! My joys are immortal, I stand on the mount!

CHORUS.

Hallelujah, I'll sing unto Jesus our King, The heart's richest tribute of praise will I bring.

110. Accepted in the Beloved.

1. All praise to the Lamb! now accepted I am,
Through faith in the Saviour's adorable name.

CHO.—*Hallelujah, 'tis done! I believe on the Son,
I am saved by the blood of the Crucified One.*

2. In him I confide, for his blood is applied;
For me he hath suffered, for me he hath died.—*Cho.*

3. No doubt doth arise now to darken the skies,
Or hide for a moment my Lord from mine eyes.—*Cho.*

4. In him I am blest, and I lean on his breast,
And lo! in his wounds I continue to rest.—*Cho.*

Copyright, 1873, by T. C. O'KANE.

111. Triumph By and By.

"I press toward the mark."—PHIL. 3:14.

Dr. C. R. BLACKALL. H. R. PALMER.

1. The prize is set be-fore us, To win, his words implore us,
2. We'll fol-low where he lead-eth, We'll pasture where he feed-eth,
3. Our home is bright a-bove us, No tri-als dark to move us,

The eye of God is o'er us, From on high, from on high; His loving
We'll yield to him who pleadeth From on high, from on high; Then naught from
But Jesus, dear, to love us, There on high, there on high; We'll give him

tones are call-ing, While sin is dark, ap-pall-ing; 'Tis Je-sus
him shall sev-er, Our hope shall brighten ev-er, And faith shall
best en-deav-or, And praise his name for-ev-er; His precious

CHORUS.

gen-tly call-ing, He is nigh, he is nigh.
fail us nev-er, He is nigh, he is nigh. By and by we shall
ones can nev-er, Nev-er die, nev-er die.

meet him, By and by we shall greet him, And with Jesus reign in

By permission.

Triumph By and By. Concluded.

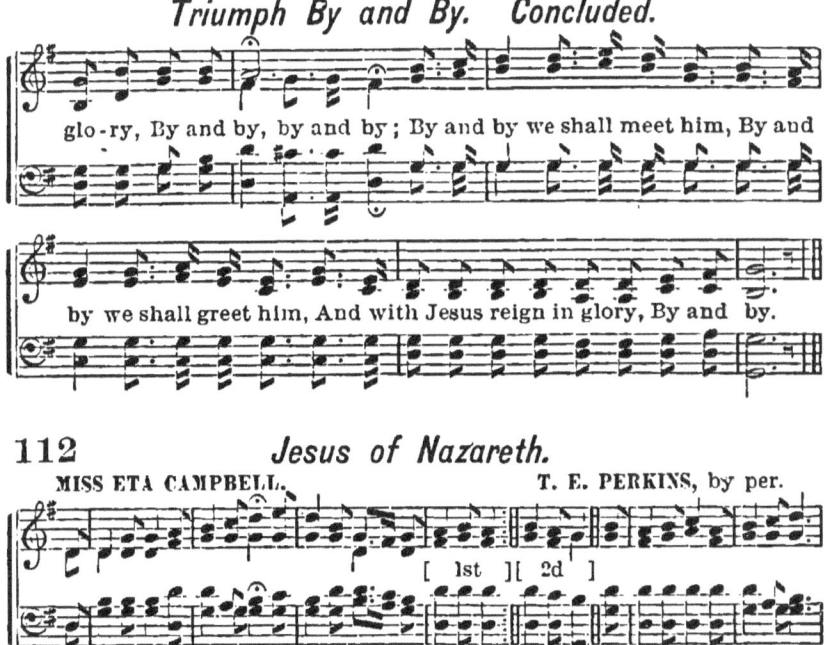

glo-ry, By and by, by and by; By and by we shall meet him, By and by we shall greet him, And with Jesus reign in glory, By and by.

112 Jesus of Nazareth.

MISS ETA CAMPBELL.   T. E. PERKINS, by per.

1 What means this eager, anxious throng,
Which moves with busy haste along;
These wondrous gath'rings day by day?
What means this strange commotion, pray?
‖:In accents hushed the throng reply,
"Jesus of Nazareth passeth by.":‖

2 Who is this Jesus? Why should he
The city move so mightily?
A passing stranger, has he skill
To move the multitude at will?
‖: Again the stirring tones reply,
"Jesus of Nazareth passeth by.":‖

3 Jesus! 'tis he who once below
Man's pathway trod 'mid pain and woe;
And burdened ones, where'er he came,
Brought out their sick, and deaf, and lame,
‖:The blind rejoice to hear the cry:
"Jesus of Nazareth passeth by.":‖

4 Again he comes! From place to place
His holy footprints we can trace.
He pauseth at our threshold—nay,
He enters—condescends to stay.
‖:Shall we not gladly raise the cry:
"Jesus of Nazareth passeth by?":‖

5 Ho! all ye heavy-laden, come;
Here's pardon, comfort, rest, and home.
Ye wanderers from a Father's face,
Return, accept his proffered grace.
‖:Ye tempted ones, there's refuge nigh:
"Jesus of Nazareth passeth by.":‖

6 But if you still this call refuse,
And all his wondrous love abuse,
Soon will he sadly from you turn,
Your bitter prayer for pardon spurn.
"Too late! too late!" will be the cry:
"Jesus of Nazareth *has passed by*.":‖

113. There'll be Joy by and by.

"Joy cometh in the morning."—Ps. 30: 5.

Mrs. E. C. ELLSWORTH.   R. LOWRY.

1. Tho' the night be dark and dreary, Tho' the way be long and weary, Morn shall bring thee light and cheer; Child, look up, the dawn is near.
2. Tho' thine eyes are sad with weeping, Thro' the night thy vigils keeping, God shall wipe thy tears away, Turn thy darkness into day.
3. Tho' thy spir-it faints with fasting Thro' the hours so slow-ly wasting, Morn shall bring a glorious feast, Thou shalt sit an honored guest.

CHORUS.
There'll be joy by and by, There'll be joy by and by; In the dawning of the morning, There'll be joy by and by.

From Welcome Tidings by Permission of Biglow & Main.

114. The Streets of the City.

1 When we reach the golden city,
  When we pass the pearly gate,
  Where our friends who went before us
  For our coming watch and wait.
Cho. We will walk in the streets of the
  With our loved ones gone before; [City,
  We will sit on the banks of the river,
  We will meet to part no more.

2 Here our happy hearts already
  Taste by faith the bliss of heaven,
  To our hungry souls the manna
  From above is freely given.

3 Then we'll gladly wait a little,
  Gladly still our burdens bear;
  Soon we'll hear our Savior's "Welcome;"
  Soon a crown of glory wear.

116. Strike for the Victory.

Rev. F. DENISON.　　　　　　T. C. O'KANE.

1. Wake from in-temp-er-ance! Hear ye mercy's song! Rouse from your festal trance! Grasp the arm that's strong. Strike for the vic-to-ry!
2. List to the trumpet call, Sweet as angel voice; Haste ere you down shall fall, Make to-day your choice.
3. Turn from the charmer's way, Fly the viper's breath; Hear now the Sav-ior say, "I will save from death."
4. Sund-er the chains of sin, Now's the hour of life; Trusting a crown to win, Nobly meet the strife.

Chorus. Dash to earth the cup! Christ gives us liberty, Lift his banner up!

117. Our God is Marching On.

1 The light of truth is breaking,
　On the mountain tops it gleams;
　Let it flash along our valleys,
　Let it glitter on our streams,
　Until all our land awakens
　In its flush of golden beams.
　　　　　Our God, etc.

2 From morning's early watches
　Till the setting of the sun
　We will never flag nor falter
　In the work we have begun,
　Till the forts have all surrendered,
　And the victory is won.
　　　　　Our God, etc.

3 We wield no carnal weapons,
　And we hurl no fiery dart;
　But with words of love and reason
　We are sure to win the heart,
　And persuade the poor transgressor
　To prefer the better part.
　　　　　Our God, etc.

4 Our strength is in Jehovah,
　And our cause is in his care;
　With almighty arms to help us
　We have faith to do and dare,
　While confiding in the promise,
　That the Lord will answer prayer.
　　　　　Our God, etc.

118 "Lovest Thou Me?"

119 **To Every One a Work.**

1 If you can not be a watchman,
  Standing high on Zion's wall,
Pointing out the path to heaven,
  Offering life and peace to all,
With your prayers and with your bounties,
  You can do what God demands;
You can be like faithful Aaron,
  Holding up the prophet's hands

2 If among the older people,
  You may not be apt to teach,
"Feed my lambs," said Christ, our shepherd,
  Place the food within their reach;
And it may be, that the children
  You have led with trembling hand
Will be found among your jewels
  When you reach the better land.

120. Prospect.

CHARLES WESLEY. — Harmonized by **T. C. O'K.**

1. And let this feeble body fail, And let it faint or die;
   My soul shall quit this mournful vale, And soar to worlds on high:
   Shall join the disembodied saints, And find its long sought rest,—
   That only bliss for which it pants, In the Redeemer's breas'

2. In hope of that immortal crown
   I now the cross sustain,
   And gladly wander up and down,
   And smile at toil and pain;
   I suffer on my threescore years,
   Till my Deliv'rer come,
   And wipe away his servant's tears,
   And take his exile home.

3. O what are all my suff'rings here,
   If, Lord, thou count me meet
   With that enraptured host t' appear,
   And worship at thy feet!
   Give joy or grief, give ease or pain,
   Take life or friends away,
   But let me find them all again
   In that eternal day.

121. Only Jesus Crucified.

WESLEY. — **W. H. OAKLEY.**

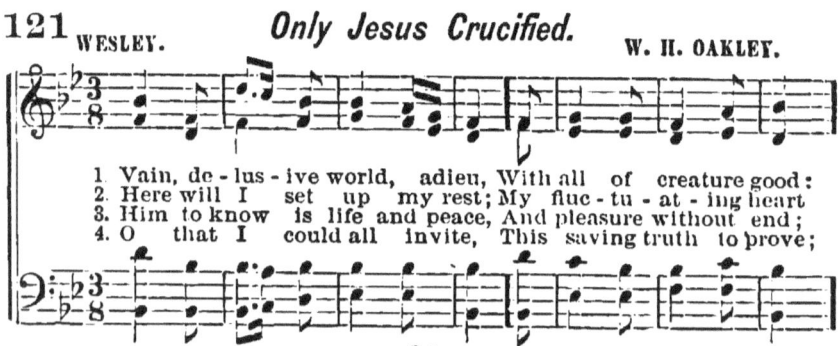

1. Vain, de-lus-ive world, adieu, With all of creature good:
2. Here will I set up my rest; My fluc-tu-at-ing heart
3. Him to know is life and peace, And pleasure without end;
4. O that I could all invite, This saving truth to prove;

Only Jesus Crucified. Concluded.

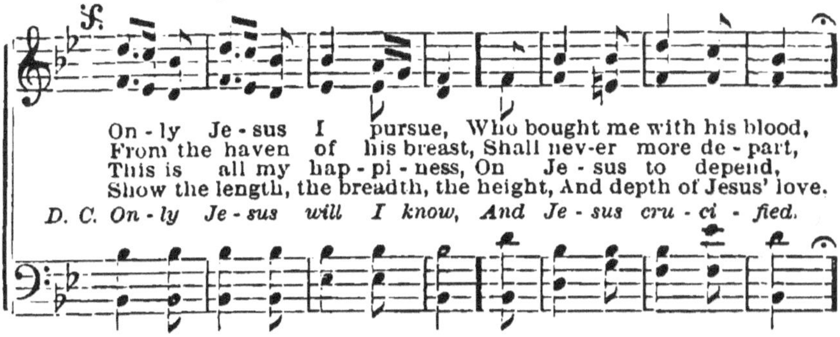

On-ly Je-sus I pursue, Who bought me with his blood,
From the haven of his breast, Shall nev-er more de-part,
This is all my hap-pi-ness, On Je-sus to depend,
Show the length, the breadth, the height, And depth of Jesus' love.

D. C. On-ly Je-sus will I know, And Je-sus cru-ci-fied.

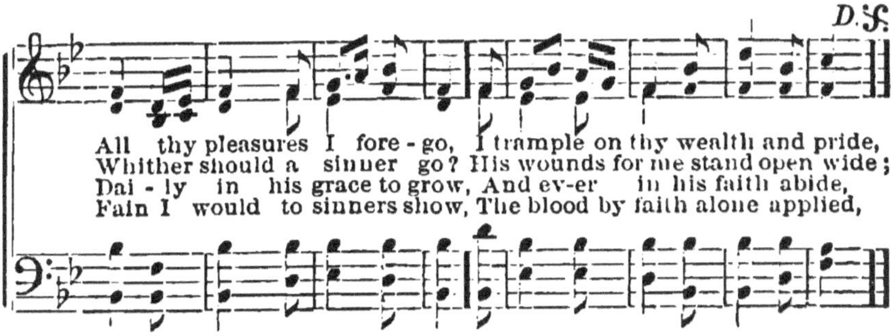

All thy pleasures I fore-go, I trample on thy wealth and pride,
Whither should a sinner go? His wounds for me stand open wide;
Dai-ly in his grace to grow, And ev-er in his faith abide,
Fain I would to sinners show, The blood by faith alone applied,

122 And can it Be?
Rev. CHAS. WESLEY.

1 And can it be that I should gain
  An int'rest in the Savior's blood?
Died he for me, who caus'd his pain?
  For me, who him to death pursued?
Amazing love! how can it be
  That thou, my Lord, shouldst die for me?

2 'T is myst'ry all, th' Immortal dies!
  Who can explore his strange design?
In vain the first-born seraph tries
  To sound the depths of love divine;
'T is mercy all! let earth adore:
  Let angel minds inquire no more.

3 He left his Father's throne above;
  (So free, so infinite his grace!)
Emptied himself of all but love,
  And bled for Adam's helpless race;
'T is mercy all, immense and free,
  For oh, my God, it found out me!

4 No condemnation now I dread;
  Jesus, with all in him, is mine;
Alive in him, my living head,
  And clothed in righteousness divine,
Bold I approach th' eternal throne
  And claim the crown thro' Christ my own.

3 Fully then trusted I in Jesus,
And oh, what a joy came to me;
My heart was filled with praises,
For he saved a poor sinner like me.
No longer in darkness I'm walking,
For the light is shining on me,
And now unto others I'm telling
How he saved a poor sinner like me.

Copyright, 1878, by JOHN R. SWENEY.

124. The Joy of Service.

Rev. J. B. ATCHISON. Har. by T. C. O'KANE.

1. O Christ, thou art my treasure! To work with thee is pleasure
 'Tis joy beyond all measure [omit . . . .] To
2. O may I ne'er grow weary Tho' rough the way and dreary,
 The end I know is cheery [omit . . . .] 'Tis
3. Tho' tempest-tossed and driven, We soon shall reach the haven,
 And there is rest in heaven [omit . . . .] Sweet

CHORUS.

win lost souls to thee.
joy for ev-er-more.   By and by we will rest with thee in
rest for ev-er-more.   And to thee will e-ter-nal praise be

heaven, When from our earth-toil riven;
giv-en, [omit . . . .] O Jesus, King of Kings!

125. Whiter than Snow.

1 Dear Jesus, I long to be perfectly whole;
I want thee forever to live in my soul;
Break down every idol, cast out every foe;
Now wash me, and I shall be whiter than snow.

CHO.—*Whiter than snow, yes, whiter than snow,
Now wash me, and I shall be whiter than snow.*

2 Dear Jesus, thou seest I patiently wait;
Come now, and within me a new heart create;
To those who have sought thou never saidst No;
Now wash me, and I shall be whiter than snow.

3 Dear Jesus, let nothing unholy remain;
Apply thine own blood and extract every stain;
To have this blest cleansing I all things forego;
Now wash me, and I shall be whiter than snow.

"My Ain Countrie."

Harmonized by T. C. O'K.

1. I am far frae my hame, an' I'm wea-ry af-tenwhiles,
I'll ne'er be fu' con-tent, un- - til my een do see
D.C. But these sichts an' these soun's will as naething be to me,

For the lang'd-for hame-bringing, an' my Father's welcome smiles.
The gowden gates of heav-en an' my . . . .
When I hear the an-gels singing in my . . . .

ain countrie. { The earth is deck'd with flow'rs, mony-tinted, fresh and gay;
ain countrie. { The birdies warble blithely, for my Father made them sae:

2 I've his gude word of promise that some gladsome day the King
To his ain royal palace his banished hame will bring.
Wi' een an' wi' heart running owre, we shall see
"The King in his beauty," an' our ain countrie.
My sins hae been mony, an' my sorrows hae been sair;
But there they'll never vex me nor be remembered mair:
His bluid hath made me white, an' his hand shall dry my een,
When he brings me hame at last to my ain countrie.

3 Like a bairn to its mither, a wee birdie to its nest,
I wad fain now be ganging unto my Savior's breast,
For he gathers in his bosom even witless lambs like me,
An' "carries them himself" to his ain countrie.
He's faithfu' that has promised, he'll surely come again,
He'll keep his tryst wi' me, at what hour I dinna ken:
But he bids me still to wait, an' ready aye to be
To gang at ony moment, to my ain countrie.

4 So I'm watching aye, and singing o' my hame as I wait,
For the soun'ing o' his footfa' this side the gowden gate,
God gie his grace to ilk ane wha listens noo to me,
That we a' may gang in gladness to our ain countrie.
I'm far frae my hame an' I'm weary aftenwhiles,
For the lang'd-for hame-bringing, an' my Father's welcome smiles.
I'll ne'er be fu' content, until my een do see
The gowden gates of heaven, an' my ain countrie.

127. Guide.

M. M. WELLS.

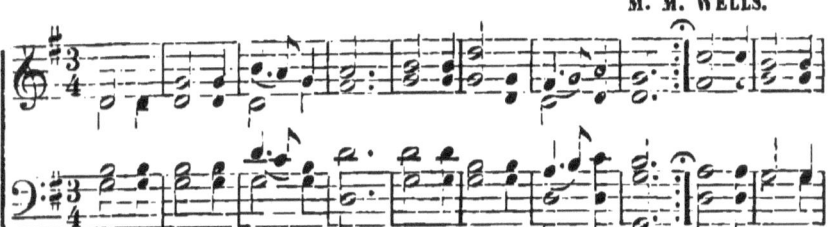

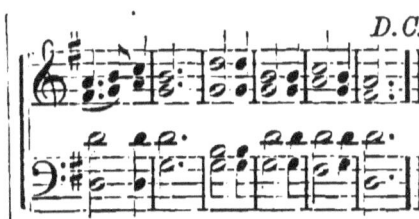

1 Holy Spirit, faithful Guide,
  Ever near the Christian's side,
  Gently lead us by the hand,
  Pilgrims in a desert land.
  Weary souls fore'er rejoice,
  While they hear that sweetest voice,
  Whisp'ring softly, wanderer, come!
  Follow me, I'll guide thee home.

2 Ever present, truest friend,
  Ever near, thine aid to lend.
  Leave us not to doubt and fear,
  Groping on in darkness drear.
  When the storms are raging sore,
  Hearts grow faint and hopes give o'er,
  Whisper softly, wanderer, come!
  Follow me, I'll guide thee home.

3 When our days of toil shall cease,
  Waiting still for sweet release,
  Nothing left but heaven and prayer,
  Wond'ring if our names are there;
  Wading deep the dismal flood,
  Pleading naught but Jesus' blood;
  Whisper softly, wanderer, come!
  Follow me, I'll guide thee home.

128. America.

Words by S. F. SMITH.

1 My country, 't is of thee,
  Sweet land of liberty,
    Of thee I sing;
  Land where my fathers died,
  Land of the pilgrim's pride,
  From ev'ry mountain side
    Let freedom ring.

2 My native country, thee,
  Land of the noble free,
    Thy name I love;
  I love thy rocks and rills,
  Thy woods and templed hills,
  My heart with rapture thrills
    Like that above.

3 Let music swell the breeze,
  And ring from all the trees
    Sweet freedom's song;
  Let mortal tongues awake,
  Let all that breathe partake,
  Let rocks their silence break,
    The sound prolong.

4 Our father's God, to thee,
  Author of liberty,
    To thee we sing;
  Long may our land be bright,
  With freedom's holy light;
  Protect us by thy might,
    Great God, our king.

129. The Star of Bethlehem.

1 When marshaled on the nightly plain,
   The glittering host bestud the sky;
One star alone of all the train
   Can fix the sinner's wandering eye.
Hark! hark! to God the chorus breaks,
   From every host, from every gem:
But one alone, the Savior speaks—
   It is the Star of Bethlehem.

2 Once on the raging seas I rode;
   The storm was loud, the night was dark,
The ocean yawned, and rudely blowed
   The wind that toss'd my found'ring bark.
Deep horror then my vitals froze;
   Death-struck, I ceased the tide to stem;
When suddenly a star arose—
   It was the Star of Bethlehem.

3 It was my guide, my life, my all;
   It bade my dark foreboding cease;
And, thro' the storm and danger's thrall,
   It led me to the port of peace.
Now, safely moored, my perils o'er,
   I'll sing, first in night's diadem,
Forever, and forever more,
   The Star! the Star of Bethlehem!

130. Bartimeus.

1 God is love, his mercy brightens
   All the path in which we move;
Bliss he grants, and woe he lightens;
   God is wisdom, God is love.

2 Chance and change are busy ever;
   Worlds decay and ages move,
But his mercy waneth never;
   God is wisdom, God is love.

3 He our earthly cares entwineth
   With his comforts from above;
Every-where his glory shineth;
   God is wisdom, God is love.

131. Duane Street.

Rev. GEORGE COLES.

1 Jesus, my all, to heaven is gone,
  He, whom I fix my hopes upon;
  His track I see, and I'll pursue
  The narrow way till him I view.
  The way the holy prophets went—
  The road that leads from banishment,—
  The King's highway of holiness,
  I'll go, for all his paths are peace.

2 This is the way I long have sought,
  And mourned because I found it not;
  My grief a burden long has been,
  Because I was not saved from sin.
  The more I strove against its power,
  I felt its weight and guilt the more;
  Till late I heard my Savior say,
  Come hither, soul, I am the way.

3 Lo! glad I come; and thou, blest Lamb,
  Shalt take me to thee as I am;
  Nothing but sin have I to give—
  Nothing but love shall I receive.
  Then will I tell to sinners round
  What a dear Savior I have found;
  I'll point to thy redeeming blood,
  And say, Behold the way to God.

132. Rathbun.

1 In the cross of Christ I glory,
    Towering o'er the wrecks of time;
  All the light of sacred story
    Gathers round its head sublime.

2 When the woes of life o'ertake me,
    Hopes deceive and fears annoy,
  Never shall the Cross forsake me;
    Lo! it glows with peace and joy.

3 When the sun of bliss is beaming Light and love upon my way, From the Cross the radiance streaming, Adds new luster to the day.

133. Deliverance Will Come.

REV. W. McDONALD.   Harmonized by T. C. O'K.

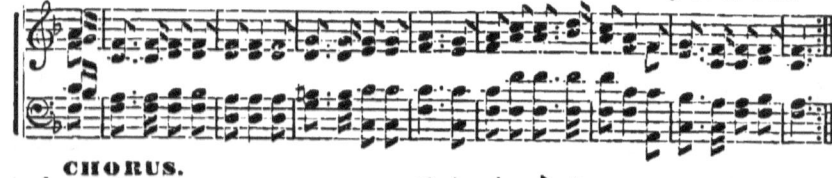

CHORUS.

1 I saw a way-worn trav'ler,
  In tattered garments clad,
And, struggling up the mountain,
  It seemed that he was sad.
His back was laden heavy,
  His strength was almost gone,
Yet he shouted as he journeyed,
  "Deliverance will come!"
    CHORUS.
  Then palms of victory,
    Crowns of glory,
  Palms of victory
    I shall wear.

2 The summer sun was shining,
  The sweat was on his brow,
His garments worn and dusty,
  His step seemed very slow:
But he kept pressing onward,
  For he was wending home,
Still shouting as he journeyed,
  "Deliverance will come!"

3 I saw him in the evening,
  The sun was bending low,
He'd overtopped the mountain
  And reached the vale below:
He saw the golden city,—
  His everlasting home,—
And shouted loud, Hosanna,
  "Deliverance will come!"

4 I heard the song of triumph
  They sang upon that shore,
Saying, Jesus has redeemed us
  To suffer nevermore:
Then, casting his eyes backward
  On the race which he had run,
He shouted loud, "Hosanna,
  Deliverance has come!"

134. Let Me Go.

1 Let me go where saints are going,
  To the mansions of the blest;
Let me go where my Redeemer
  Has prepared his people's rest.
I would gain those realms of brightness—
  Where they dwell for evermore;
I would join the friends that wait me
  Over on the other shore.

    CHORUS.
Let me go, 'tis Jesus calls me;
  Let me gain the realms of day;
Bear me over angel pinions,
  Longs my soul to be away.

2 Let me go where none are weary,
  Where is raised no wail of woe;
Let me go and bathe my spirit
  In the raptures angels know;
Let me go, for bliss eternal
  Lures my soul away, away,
And the victor's song triumphant
  Thrills my heart—I can not stay.

3 Let me go where tears and sighing
  Are for evermore unknown,
Where the joyous songs of glory
  Call me to a happier home.
Let me go—I'd cease this dying,
  I would gain life's fairer plains;
Let me join the myriad harpers,
  Let me chant their rapturous strains.

135. The Night Cometh.

1 Work, for the night is coming,
  Work through the morning hours;
Work while the dew is sparkling,
  Work 'mid springing flowers;
Work when the day grows brighter,
  Work in the glowing sun;
Work, for the night is coming,
  When man's work is done.

2 Work, for the night is coming,
  Work through the sunny noon;
Fill brightest hours with labor,
  Rest comes sure and soon.
Give every flying minute
  Something to keep in store;
Work, for the night is coming,
  When man works no more.

3 Work, for the night is coming,
  Under the sunset skies;
While their bright tints are glowing,
  Work, for the daylight flies.
Work till the last beam fadeth,
  Fadeth to shine no more;
Work while the night is darkening,
  When man's work is o'er.

Duke Street. L. M.

136 The Savior's Kingdom.
1 Jesus shall reign where'er the sun
Doth his successive journeys run;
His kingdom spread from shore to shore,
Till moon shall wax and wane no more.

2 From north to south the princes
To pay their homage at his feet; [meet
While western empires own their Lord,
And savage tribes attend his word.

3 People and realms of every tongue
Dwell on his love with sweetest song,
And infant voices shall proclaim
Their early blessings on his Name.

137 Joy of Worship.
1 Great God, attend, while Zion sings
The joy that from thy presence springs;
To spend one day with thee on earth
Exceeds a thousand days of mirth.

2 God is our sun, he makes our day;
God is our shield, he guards our way
From all assaults of hell and sin,
From foes without and foes within.

3 All needful grace will God bestow,
And crown that grace with glory too;
He gives us all things, and withholds
No real good from upright souls.

138 Love passing Knowledge.
1 Of him who did salvation bring,
I could forever think and sing;
Arise, ye needy,—he 'll relieve;
Arise, ye guilty, he 'll forgive.

2 'Tis thee I love, for thee alone
I shed my tears and make my moan;
Where'er I am, where'er I move,
I meet the object of my love.

3 Insatiate to this spring I fly;
I drink, and yet am ever dry:
Ah! who against thy charms is proof?
Ah! who that loves, can love enough?

139 The Church.
1 Jesus, from whom all blessings flow,
Great Builder of thy Church below,
If now thy Spirit moves my breast,
Hear, and fulfill thine own request.

2 The few that truly call thee Lord,
And wait thy sanctifying word,
And thee their utmost Savior own—
Unite and perfect them in one.

3 O let them all thy mind express,
Stand forth thy chosen witnesses;
Thy power unto salvation show,
And perfect holiness below.

140 Spiritual Baptism.
1 O Spirit of the living God,
In all thy plenitude of grace,
Where'er the foot of man hath trod,
Descend on our apostate race.

2 Give tongues of fire and hearts of love,
To preach the reconciling word;
Give power and unction from above,
Where'er the joyful sound is heard.

3 Baptize the nations; far and nigh
The triumphs of the cross record;
The name of Jesus glorify
Till every kindred call him Lord.

141 Following the Savior.
1 O thou, to whose all-searching sight
The darkness shineth as the light,
Search, prove my heart, it pants for thee;
O burst these bonds, and set it free.

2 Savior, where'er thy steps I see,
Dauntless, untired, I follow thee;
O let thy hand support me still,
And lead me to thy holy hill.

3 If rough and thorny be the way,
My strength proportion to my day;
Till toil, and grief, and pain shall cease,
Where all is calm, and joy, and peace.

Hursley. L. M.

142

1 Sun of my soul, thou Savior dear,
It is not night if thou art near:
O may no earth-born cloud arise
To hide thee from thy servant's eyes.

2 Abide with me from morn till eve,
For without thee I can not live;
Abide with me when night is nigh,
For without thee I dare not die.

3 Watch by the sick, enrich the poor,
With blessings from thy boundless store;
Be every mourner's sleep to night,
Like infant's slumbers, pure and light.

4 Come near and bless us when we wake,
Ere thro' the world our way we take,
Till in the ocean of thy love
We lose ourselves in heaven above.

143 Living Redeemer.

1 I know that my Redeemer lives—
What joy the blest assurance gives!
He lives, he lives, who once was dead;
He lives, my everlasting Head!

2 He lives, to bless me with his love;
He lives, to plead for me above;
He lives, my hungry soul to feed;
He lives, to help in time of need.

3 He lives—all glory to his name;
He lives my Savior, still the same:
What joy the blest assurance gives,—
I know that my Redeemer lives.

144 Protection.

1 Thus far the Lord hath led me on—
Thus far his power prolongs my days; [known
And every evening shall make
Some fresh memorial of his grace.

2 Much of my time has run to waste,
And I, perhaps, am near my home;
But he forgives my follies past, [come.
And gives me strength for days to

3 I lay my body down to sleep;
Peace is the pillow for my head;
While well-appointed angels keep
Their watchful stations round my bed.

Hamburg. L. M.

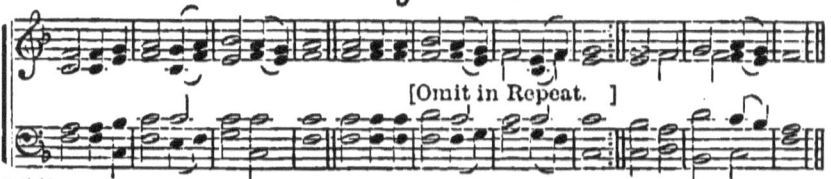

[Omit in Repeat.]

145 The Only Plea.

1 Just as I am, without one plea,
But that thy blood was shed for me,
And that thou bidd'st me come to thee,
  O Lamb of God! I come, I come!

2 Just as I am, poor, wretched, blind,
Sight, riches, healing of the mind,
Yea, all I need, in thee to find,
  O Lamb of God! I come, I come!

3 Just as I am—thou wilt receive;
Wilt welcome, pardon, cleanse, relieve:
Because thy promise I believe,
  O Lamb of God! I come, I come!

146 Entirely Thine.

1 Lord, I am thine, entirely thine,
Purchased and saved by blood divine;
With full consent thine I would be,
And own thy sovereign right in me.

2 Thine would I live—thine would I
Be thine through all eternity; [die;
The vow is past beyond repeal,
And now I set the solemn seal.

3 Here, at that cross where flows the blood
That bought my guilty soul for God—
Thee, my new Master, now I call,
And consecrate to thee my all.

Rockingham. L. M.

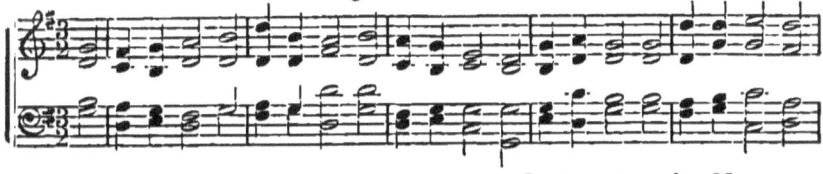

Retreat. L. M.

147   Saving Faith.

1 We have no outward righteousness,
  No merits or good works, to plead ;
  We only can be saved by grace ;
    Thy grace, O Lord, is free indeed.

2 Save us by grace, thro' faith alone,
  A faith thou must thyself impart ;
  A faith that would by works be shown,
    A faith that purifies the heart:

3 This is the faith we humbly seek,
  The faith in thy all-cleansing blood;
  That faith which doth for sinners [speak,
    O let it speak us up to God !

148   The Light Yoke.

1 O that my load of sin were gone !
  O that I could at last submit,
  At Jesus' feet to lay it down—
    To lay my soul at Jesus' feet.

2 Break off the yoke of inbred sin,
  And fully set my spirit free ;
  I can not rest till pure within,—
    Till I am wholly lost in thee.

3 Fain would I learn of thee, my God;
  Thy light and easy burden prove ;
  The cross all stain'd with hallow'd [blood,
    The labor of thy dying love.

4 I would, but thou must give the power;
  My heart from every sin release ;
  Bring near, bring near the joyful hour,
    And fill me with thy perfect peace.

149   Blessed Sleep.

1 Asleep in Jesus ! blessed sleep !
  From which none ever wake to weep;
  A calm and undisturbed repose,
    Unbroken by the last of foes.

2 Asleep in Jesus ! peaceful rest !
  Whose waking is supremely blest;
  No fear, no woe, shall dim that hour,
    Which manifests the Savior's power.

3 Asleep in Jesus ! oh, for me
  May such a blissful refuge be !
  Securely shall my ashes lie,
    And wait the summons from on high.

150   The Mercy-Seat.

1 From every stormy wind that blows,
  From every swelling tide of woes,
  There is a calm, a sure retreat;
    'Tis found beneath the mercy-seat.

2 There is a place, where Jesus sheds
  The oil of gladness on our heads;
  A place than all besides more sweet,—
    It is the blood-bought mercy-seat.

3 There is a scene where spirits blend,
  Where friend holds fellowship with friend,
  Tho' sunder'd far, by faith they meet
    Around one common mercy-seat.

4 There, there on eagles' wings we soar,
  And sin and sense molest no more ;
  And heaven comes down our souls to greet,
    While glory crowns the mercy-seat.

Arlington. C. M.

Cross and Crown.

151. The Spirit Sought.

1 Come, Holy Spirit, heavenly Dove,
  With all thy quick'ning powers;
Kindle a flame of sacred love
  In these cold hearts of ours.

2 Father, and shall we ever live
  At this poor dying rate—
Our love so faint, so cold to thee,
  And thine to us so great?

3 Come, Holy Spirit, heavenly Dove,
  With all thy quick'ning powers;
Come, shed abroad a Savior's love,
  And that shall kindle ours.

152 The Word.

1 Father of mercies, in thy Word
  What endless glory shines!
Forever be thy name adored
  For these celestial lines.

2 Here the Redeemer's welcome voice
  Spreads heavenly peace around;
And life, and everlasting joys,
  Attend the blissful sound.

3 Oh, may these heavenly pages be
  Our ever dear delight;
And still new beauties may we see,
  And still increasing light.

4 Divine Instructor, gracious Lord,
  Be thou forever near;
Teach us to love thy sacred word,
  And view the Savior there.

153 Cross and Crown.

1 Must Jesus bear the cross alone,
  And all the world go free?
No: there's a cross for every one,
  And there's a cross for me.

2 How happy are the saints above
  Who once went sorrowing here;
But now they taste unmingled love,
  And joy without a tear.

3 The consecrated cross I'll bear,
  Till death shall set me free,
And then go home my crown to wear,
  For there's a crown for me!

154 Gratitude.

1 When all thy mercies, oh, my God,
  My rising soul surveys,
Transported with the view, I'm lost
  In wonder, love, and praise.

2 O how can words with equal warmth
  The gratitude declare,
That glows within my ravish'd heart?
  But thou canst read it there.

3 Thro' every period of my life,
  Thy goodness I'll pursue;
And after death, in distant worlds,
  The pleasing theme renew.

4 Thro' all eternity to thee
  A grateful song I'll raise,
But, oh! eternity's too short
  To utter all thy praise.

Azmon. C. M.

Siloam. C. M.

155 A Closer Walk.

1 Oh, for a closer walk with God!
  A calm and heavenly frame;
  A light to shine upon the road
  That leads me to the Lamb.

2 The dearest idol I have known,
  Whate'er that idol be,
  Help me to tear it from thy throne,
  And worship only thee.

3 So shall my walk be close with God,
  Calm and serene my frame;
  So purer light shall mark the road
  That leads me to the Lamb.

156 Not Ashamed.

1 I'm not ashamed to own my Lord,
  Or to defend his cause;
  Maintain the honor of his word,—
  The glory of his cross.

2 Jesus, my God! I know his name;
  His name is all my trust;
  Nor will he put my soul to shame,
  Nor let my hope be lost.

3 Firm as his throne his promise
  And he can well secure   [stands,
  What I've committed to his hands,
  Till the decisive hour.

4 Then will he own my worthless
  Before his Father's face,   [name
  And in the New Jerusalem
  Appoint my soul a place.

157 Early Piety.

1 By cool Siloam's shady rill,
  How sweet the lily grows!
  How sweet the breath, beneath the
  Of Sharon's dewy rose!   [hill,

2 Lo! such the child whose early feet
  The paths of peace have trod—
  Whose secret heart, with influence
  Is upward drawn to God.   [sweet,

3 Oh, thou who givest life and breath!
  We seek thy grace alone,
  In childhood, manhood, age, and
  To keep us still thine own.   [death,

158 Final Triumph.

1 Am I a soldier of the cross,—
  A foll'wer of the Lamb,
  And shall I fear to own his cause,
  Or blush to speak his name?

2 Since I must fight if I would reign,
  Increase my courage, Lord;
  I'll bear the toil, endure the pain,
  Supported by thy word.

3 Thy saints in all this glorious war
  Shall conquer, though they die:
  They see the triumph from afar,—
  By faith they bring it nigh.

4 When that illustrious day shall rise,
  And all thy armies shine
  In robes of vict'ry through the skies,
  The glory shall be thine.

Coronation. C. M.

159   **Exultant Praise.**

1 Oh, for a thousand tongues to sing
   My great Redeemer's praise;
The glories of my God and King,
   The triumphs of his grace.

2 My gracious Master, and my God,
   Assist me to proclaim—
To spread thro' all the earth abroad,
   The honors of thy name.

3 Jesus! the name that charms our
   That bids our sorrows cease; [fears,
'T is music in the sinner's ears,
   'T is life, and health, and peace.

160   **Lord of All.**

1 All hail the power of Jesus' name!
   Let angels prostrate fall;
Bring forth the royal diadem,
   And crown him Lord of all.

2 Let every kindred, every tribe,
   On this terrestrial ball,
To him all majesty ascribe,
   And crown him Lord of all.

3 Oh, that with yonder sacred throng
   We at his feet may fall!
We'll join the everlasting song,
   And crown him Lord of all.

Harp. C. M.

[Omit in Repeat. . .]

161   **Overcoming Faith.**

1 Oh for a faith that will not shrink,
   Though press'd by every foe,
That will not tremble on the brink
   Of any earthly woe;—

2 A faith that shines more bright and
   When tempests rage without; [clear
That when in danger knows no fear,
   In darkness feels no doubt;—

3 A faith that keeps the narrow way
   Till life's last hour is fled,
And with a pure and heavenly ray
   Illumes a dying bed.

4 Lord, give us such a faith as this,
   And then, whate'er may come,
We'll taste, e'en here, the hallow'd
   Of an eternal home.   [bliss

162   **A Perfect Heart.**

1 Oh for a heart to praise my God,
   A heart from sin set free;—
A heart that always feels thy blood,
   So freely spilt for me.

2 A heart resign'd, submissive, meek,
   My great Redeemer's throne;
Where only Christ is heard to speak,
   Where Jesus reigns alone.

3 A heart in every thought renewed,
   And full of love divine;
Perfect, and right, and pure, and good,
   A copy, Lord, of thine.

4 Thy nature, gracious Lord, impart;
   Come quickly from above;
Write thy new name upon my heart,
   Thy new, best name of Love.

Varina.

163 The Heavenly Canaan.

1 There is a land of pure delight,
   Where saints immortal reign;
Infinite day excludes the night,
   And pleasures banish pain.
There everlasting spring abides,
   And never-with'ring flowers;
Death, like a narrow sea, divides
   This heavenly land from ours.

2 Sweet fields beyond the swelling flood
   Stand dressed in living green;
So to the Jews old Canaan stood,
   While Jordan roll'd between.
Could we but climb where Moses stood,
   And view the landscape o'er,
Not Jordan's stream, nor death's cold flood
   Should fright us from the shore.

164 Assurance of Hope.

1 How happy every child of grace,
   That knows his sins forgiven!
This earth, he cries, is not my place;
   I seek my place in heaven:
A country far from mortal sight,
   Yet, oh, by faith I see
The land of rest, the saints' delight,
   The heaven prepared for me.

2 Oh, what a blessed hope is ours!
   While here on earth we stay;
We more than taste the heavenly powers,
   And antedate that day;
We feel the resurrection near—
   Our life in Christ concealed—
And with his glorious presence here
   Our earthen vessel's filled.

Peoria.

[Omit in Repeat.]

165 Refining Fire.

1 Jesus, thine all-victorious love
   Shed in my heart abroad:
Then shall my feet no longer rove,
   Rooted and fixed in God.

2 Oh that it now from heaven might fall,
   And all my sins consume:
Come, Holy Ghost, for thee I call;
   Spirit of burning, come.

3 Refining fire, go through my heart;
   Illuminate my soul;
Scatter thy life through every part,
   And sanctify the whole.

4 My steadfast soul, from falling free,
   Shall then no longer move,
While Christ is all the world to me,
   And all my heart is love.

166 Triumphant Joy.

1 My God, the spring of all my joys,
   The life of my delights,
The glory of my brightest days,
   And comfort of my nights.

2 In darkest shades, if thou appear,
   My dawning is begun;
Thou art my soul's bright morning star,
   And thou my rising sun.

3 The opening heavens around me shine
   With beams of sacred bliss,
If Jesus shows his mercy mine,
   And whispers I am his.

4 My soul would leave this heavy clay
   At that transporting word;
Run up with joy the shining way,
   To see and praise my Lord.

St. Thomas. S. M.

Heavenly Shore.

I'm glad salvation's free; Salvation's free for you and me; I'm glad salvation's free.

167 The Church.

1 I love thy kingdom, Lord,
  The house of thine abode—
The Church our blest Redeemer saved
  With his own precious blood.

2 I love thy Church, O God!
  Her walls before thee stand
Dear as the apple of thine eye,
  And graven on thy hand.

3 For her my tears shall fall;
  For her my prayers ascend;
To her my cares and toils be given,
  Till toils and cares shall end.

4 Sure as thy truth shall last,
  To Zion shall be given
The brightest glories earth can yield,
  And brighter bliss of heaven.

168 Revival.

1 O Lord, thy work revive
  In Zion's gloomy hour,
And let our dying graces live
  By thy restoring power.

2 Oh, let thy chosen few
  Awake to earnest prayer!
Their covenant again renew,
  And walk in filial fear.

3 Now lend thy gracious ear;
  Now listen to our cry;
Oh, come and bring salvation near!
  Our souls on thee rely.

169 Free Salvation.

1 I'm glad salvation's free,
  And without price or cost;
For had it been for me to buy,
  My soul must have been lost.

2 In this cold world below,
  With none to care for me,
A pilgrim often sad and lone,
  I'm glad salvation's free.

3 Once I was blind and lost,
  Of sin and sorrow full;
But now I'm saved thro' Jesus' blood,
  I feel it in my soul.

4 And now I'm on my way
  To brighter worlds above;
I hope to triumph evermore
  Through my Redeemer's love.

170 Grace.

1 Grace! 'tis a charming sound,
  Harmonious to the ear;
Heaven with the echo shall resound,
  And all the earth shall hear.

2 Grace led my roving feet
  To tread the heavenly road;
And new supplies each hour I meet,
  While pressing on to God.

3 Grace all the work shall crown
  Through everlasting days,
And every ransomed power shall join
  In wonder, love, and praise.

Thatcher. S. M.

Laban. S. M.

171   Diligence.

1 A charge to keep I have,
  A God to glorify;
A never-dying soul to save,
  And fit it for the sky.

2 To serve the present age,
  My calling to fulfill,
Oh, may it all my powers engage,
  To do my Master's will.

3 Arm me with jealous care,
  As in thy sight to live;
And, oh, thy servant, Lord, prepare
  A strict account to give.

4 Help me to watch and pray,
  And on thyself rely,
Assured, if I my trust betray,
  I shall forever die.

172   Seed Sown.

1 Sow in the morn thy seed;
  At eve hold not thy hand;
To doubt and fear give thou no heed,
  Broadcast it o'er the land.

2 Thou knowest not which shall
  The late or early sown;   [thrive,
Grace keeps the perfect germ alive,
  When and wherever strewn.

3 Thou canst not toil in vain;
  Cold, heat, and moist, and dry,
Shall foster and mature the grain
  For garners in the sky.

173   Perseverance.

1 My soul, be on thy guard;
  Ten thousand foes arise;
The hosts of sin are pressing hard
  To draw thee from the skies.

2 Oh, watch, and fight, and pray;
  The battle ne'er give o'er;
Renew it boldly every day,
  And help divine implore.

3 Ne'er think the vict'ry won,
  Nor lay thine armor down;
The work of faith will not be done,
  Till thou obtain the crown.

4 Then persevere till death
  Shall bring thee to thy God;
He'll take thee, at thy parting breath,
  To his divine abode.

174   Throne of Grace.

1 Behold the throne of grace;
  The promise calls us near;
There Jesus shows a smiling face,
  And waits to answer prayer.

2 Thine image, Lord, bestow—
  Thy presence and thy love—
That we may serve thee here below,
  And reign with thee above.

3 Teach us to live by faith—
  Conform our wills to thine;
Let us victorious be in death,
  And then in glory shine.

Martyn. 7s.

175   **My Refuge and Salvation.**

1 Jesus, lover of my soul,
   Let me to thy bosom fly,
 While the nearer waters roll,
   While the tempest still is high.
 Hide me, oh, my Savior! hide,
   Till the storm of life is past;
 Safe into the haven guide,
   Oh, receive my soul at last.

2 Other refuge have I none;
   Hangs my helpless soul on thee;
 Leave, oh, leave me not alone!
   Still support and comfort me.
 All my trust on thee is stayed;
   All my help from thee I bring;
 Cover my defenseless head
   With the shadow of thy wing.

3 Plenteous grace with thee is found,
   Grace to cover all my sin;
 Let the healing streams abound;
   Make and keep me pure within.
 Thou of life the fountain art;
   Freely let me take of thee;
 Spring thou up within my heart;
   Rise to all eternity.

Hendon. 7s.

176   **The Precious Bible.**

1 Holy Bible! book divine!
 Precious treasure! thou art mine!
 Mine, to tell me whence I came;
 Mine, to teach me what I am;

2 Mine, to chide me when I rove;
 Mine, to show a Savior's love;
 Mine art thou to guide my feet;
 Mine, to judge, condemn, acquit;

3 Mine, to comfort in distress,
 If the Holy Spirit bless;
 Mine, to show by living faith
 Man can triumph over death;

4 Mine, to tell of joys to come,
 And the rebel sinner's doom;
 Oh, thou precious book divine!
 Precious treasure! thou art mine!

177   **For a General Blessing.**

1 Lord, we come before thee now;
 At thy feet we humbly bow;
 Oh, do not our suit disdain!
 Shall we seek thee, Lord, in vain?

2 Lord, on thee our souls depend;
 In compassion now descend;
 Fill our hearts with thy rich grace,
 Tune our lips to sing thy praise.

3 Send some message from thy word,
 That may joy and peace afford;
 Let thy Spirit now impart
 Full salvation to each heart.

4 Grant that all may seek and find
 Thee, a gracious God, and kind;
 Heal the sick, the captive free;
 Let us all rejoice in thee.

Merdin. 7s, 6s & 7s.

Horton. 7s.

178 Heavenly Glories.

1 Burst, ye emerald gates, and bring
  To my raptured vision,
All the ecstatic joys that spring
  Round the bright elysian.
Lo, we lift our longing eyes!
Break, ye intervening skies!
Sons of righteousness, arise,
Ope the gates of paradise!

2 Hark! the thrilling symphonies
  Seem, methinks, to seize us;
Join we, too, the holy lays—
  Jesus, Jesus, Jesus!
Sweetest sound in seraph's song,
Sweetest note on mortal tongue,
Sweetest carol ever sung—
Jesus, Jesus, flow along.

179 The Word Glorified.

1 Sons of God, your Savior praise!
  He the door hath opened wide;
He hath given the word of grace;
  Jesus' word is glorified.
Jesus, mighty to redeem,
He alone the work hath wrought;
Worthy is the work of him, [naught.
  Him who spake a world from

2 Saw ye not the cloud arise,
  Little as a human hand?
Now it spreads along the skies,
  Hangs o'er all the thirsty land.
Lo! the promise of a shower
Drops already from above;
But the Lord will shortly pour
All the Spirit of his love.

180 Danger of Delay.

1 Hasten, sinner, to be wise!
  Stay not for the morrow's sun;
Wisdom if you still despise,
  Harder is it to be won.

2 Hasten, mercy to implore!
  Stay not for the morrow's sun,
Lest thy season should be o'er
  Ere this evening's stage be run.

3 Hasten, sinner, to return!
  Stay not for the morrow's sun,
Lest thy lamp should fail to burn
  Ere salvation's work is done.

4 Hasten, sinner, to be blest!
  Stay not for the morrow's sun,
Lest perdition thee arrest
  Ere the morrow is begun.

181 Pilgrim's Song.

1 Children of the heavenly King,
  As we journey let us sing—
Sing our Savior's worthy praise,
Glorious in his works and ways.
We are trav'ling home to God,
In the way our fathers trod;
They are happy now, and we
Soon their happiness shall see.

2 Fear not, brethren, joyful stand
  On the borders of our land;
Jesus Christ, our Father's Son,
Bids us undismayed go on.
Lord, obediently we'll go,
Gladly leaving all below;
Only thou our leader be,
And we still will follow thee.

Missionary Hymn. 7s & 6s.

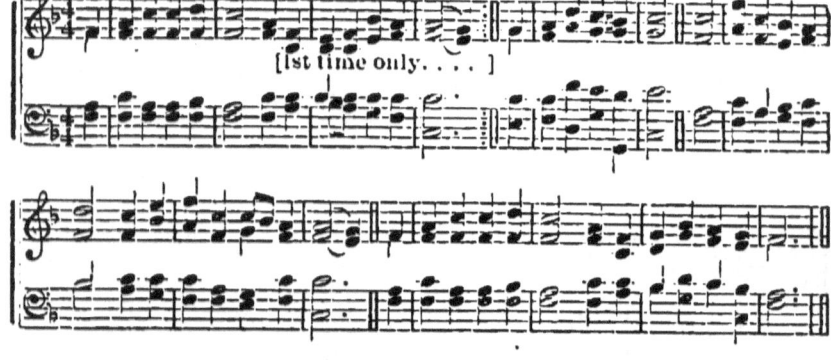

[1st time only. . . .]

Webb. 7s & 6s.

[1st time only.]

D. C.

182 Light Breaking.

1 The morning light is breaking;
  The darkness disappears;
The sons of earth are waking
  To penitential tears:
Each breeze that sweeps the ocean
  Brings tidings from afar
Of nations in commotion,
  Prepared for Zion's war.

2 Blest river of salvation,
  Pursue thy onward way;
Flow thou to every nation,
  Nor in thy richness stay:
Stay not till all the lowly
  Triumphant reach their home;
Stay not till all the holy
  Proclaim, "The Lord is come!"

183 Christian Zeal.

1 Ashamed to be a Christian,
  Afraid the world should know
I'm on my way to Zion,
  Where joys eternal flow!
Forbid it, oh, my Savior!
  That I should ever be
Afraid to wear thy color,
  Or blush to follow thee.

2 Ashamed to be a Christian,
  To love my God and King!
The fire of zeal is burning,
  My soul is on the wing.
I want a faith made perfect,
  That all the world may see,
I stand a living witness
  Of mercy, rich and free.

184 Call for Help.

1 From Greenland's icy mountains,
  From India's coral strand,
Where Afric's sunny fountains
  Roll down their golden sand,
From many an ancient river,
  From many a palmy plain,
They call us to deliver
  Their land from error's chain.

2 Shall we, whose souls are lighted
  With wisdom from on high;
Shall we to men benighted
  The lamp of life deny?
Salvation—O salvation!
  The joyful sound proclaim,
Till earth's remotest nation
  Has learned Messiah's name.

3 Waft, waft, ye winds, his story,
  And you, ye waters, roll,
Till, like a sea of glory,
  It spreads from pole to pole;
Till o'er our ransomed nature
  The Lamb for sinners slain,
Redeemer, King, Creator,
  In bliss returns to reign.

Toplady.

Oron.

185 Rock of Ages.

1 Rock of Ages, cleft for me,
Let me hide myself in thee;
Let the water and the blood,
From thy wounded side which flow'd,
Be of sin the double cure;
Save from wrath, and make me pure.

2 Could my tears forever flow—
Could my zeal no languor know—
These for sin could not atone;
Thou must save and thou alone:
In my hand no price I bring;
Simply to the cross I cling.

3 While I draw this fleeting breath,
When my eyes shall close in death,
When I rise to worlds unknown,
And behold thee on thy throne—
Rock of Ages, cleft for me,
Let me hide myself in thee.

186 The Litany.

1 By thy birth, and by thy tears;
By thy human griefs and fears;
By thy conflict in the hour
Of the subtle tempter's power—
Savior, look with pitying eye;
Savior, help me, or I die.

2 By thy lonely hour of prayer;
By the fearful conflict there;
By thy cross and dying cries;
By thy one great sacrifice—
Savior, look with pitying eye;
Savior, help me, or I die.

3 By thy triumph o'er the grave;
By thy power the lost to save;
By thy high majestic throne;
By the empire all thine own—
Savior, look with pitying eye;
Savior, help me, or I die.

187 Plea for Mercy.

1 Depth of mercy! can there be
Mercy still reserved for me?
Can my God his wrath forbear?
Me, the chief of sinners, spare?

2 I have long withstood his grace,
Long provoked him to his face;
Would not hearken to his calls;
Grieved him by a thousand falls.

3 There for me the Savior stands;
Shows his wounds and spreads his hands;
God is love! I know, I feel;
Jesus weeps, and loves me still.

188 Like Jesus.

1 I rest my soul on Jesus,
  This weary soul of mine;
His right hand me embraces;
  I on his breast recline.
I love the name of Jesus,
  Immanuel, Christ, the Lord;
Like fragrance on the breeze,
  His name abroad is poured.

2 I long to be like Jesus,
  Meek, loving, lowly, mild;
I long to be like Jesus,
  The Father's holy child;
I long to be with Jesus,
  Amid the heavenly throng,
To sing with saints his praises,
  To learn the angels' song.

Love Divine.

T. C. O'KANE.

[1st time only.]

D. C.

189   **The New Creation.**

1 Love divine, all love excelling,
  Joy of heaven to earth come down;
Fix in us thy humble dwelling;
  All thy faithful mercies crown.
Jesus, thou art all compassion,—
  Pure, unbounded love thou art;
Visit us with thy salvation;
  Enter every trembling heart.

2 Come, almighty to deliver,
  Let us all thy life receive;
Suddenly return, and never,
  Never more thy temples leave:
Thee we would be always blessing,
  Serve thee as thy hosts above,
Pray, and praise thee without ceas-
Glory in thy perfect love.   [ing,

3 Finish then thy new creation;
  Pure and spotless let us be;
Let us see thy great salvation,
  Perfectly restored in thee:
Changed from glory into glory,
  Till in heaven we take our place,—
Till we cast our crowns before thee,
  Lost in wonder, love, and praise.

190   **A Blessing Asked.**

1 Heavenly Father, grant thy bless-
    ing,
  While once more thy praise we sing;
Sinful hearts and lives confessing,
  Nothing worthy can we bring;
Yet thy book of love hath taught us,
  Thou wilt kindly bow thine ear;
For the sake of him who bought us,
  We may call, and thou wilt hear.

2 What a boon to us is given,
  Thus to lift our voice on high!
Well assured the ear of heaven
  Hears our wants, and will supply.
Weak and sinful—oh, how often
  Must we look to God alone!
For his grace our hearts to soften
  And sustain us as his own.

191   **Fount of Blessing.**

1 Come, thou fount of every blessing,
  Tune my heart to sing thy grace;
Streams of mercy, never ceasing,
  Call for songs of loudest praise.
Teach me some melodious sonnet,
  Sung by flaming tongues above;
Praise the mount—I'm fixed upon it,
  Mount of thy redeeming love.

2 Here I'll raise mine Ebenezer;
  Hither by thy help I'm come;
And I hope, by thy good pleasure,
  Safely to arrive at home.
Jesus sought me when a stranger,
  Wand'ring from the fold of God;
He, to rescue me from danger,
  Interposed his precious blood.

3 Oh, to grace, how great a debtor
  Daily I'm constrained to be!
Let thy goodness, like a fetter,
  Bind my wand'ring heart to thee.
Prone to wander, Lord, I feel it—
  Prone to leave the God I love;
Here's my heart; oh, take and seal it!
  Seal it for thy courts above.

192   **Give in Faith.**

1 Cast thy bread upon the waters,
  Thinking not 'tis thrown away;
God himself saith thou shalt gather
  It again some future day.
Cast thy bread upon the waters,
  Wildly though the billows roll;
They but aid thee as thou toilest
  Truth to spread from pole to pole.

2 Cast thy bread upon the waters;
  Why wilt thou still doubting stand?
Bounteous shall God send the harvest,
  If thou sow'st with liberal hand.
Give, then, freely of thy substance—
  O'er this cause the Lord doth reign;
Cast thy bread, and toil with patience,
  Thou shalt labor not in vain.

Disciple. 8s & 7s. Double.

193 Following Jesus.

1 Jesus, I my cross have taken,
  All to leave and follow thee;
Naked, poor, despised, forsaken,
  Thou, from hence, my all shalt be!
Perish, every fond ambition,
  All I've sought, or hoped, or known;
Yet how rich is my condition;
  God and heaven are still my own!

2 Let the world despise and leave me;
  They have left my Savior, too;
Human hearts and looks deceive me;
  Thou art not, like them, untrue.
Oh! while thou dost smile upon me,
  God of wisdom, love, and might,
Foes may hate, and friends disown me,
  Show thy face, and all is bright.

194 Joy at the Cross.

1 Sweet the moments, rich in blessing,
  Which before the cross I spend;
Life, and health, and peace possessing,
  From the sinner's dying friend.
Love and grief, my heart dividing,
  With my tears his feet I'll bathe;
Constant still, in faith abiding,
  Life deriving from his death.

2 Truly blessed is this station,
  Low before his cross to lie,
While I see divine compassion
  Beaming in his gracious eye.
Here I'll sit, forever viewing
  Mercy streaming in his blood;
Precious drops my soul bedewing,
  Plead and claim my peace with God.

Stowell. 8s & 7s.

T. C. O'KANE.

195

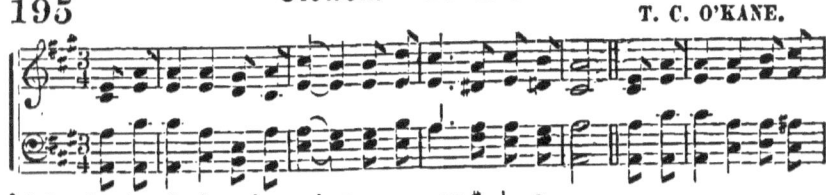

1 Silently the shades of evening
  Gather round our chapel door;
Silently they bring before us
  Faces we shall see no more.

2 Oh, the lost, the unforgotten!
  Though the world be oft forgot;
Oh, the shrouded and the lonely!
  In our hearts they perish not.

3 Living in the silent hours,
  Where our spirits only blend,
They, unlinked with earthly trouble,
  We still hoping for its end.

196 Evening Blessing.

1 Savior, breathe an evening blessing,
  Ere repose our spirits seal;
Sin and want we come confessing;
  Thou canst save and thou canst heal.

2 Tho' the night be dark and dreary,
  Darkness can not hide from thee;
Thou art he who, never weary,
  Watchest where thy people be.

3 Should swift death this night o'ertake us,
  And command us to the tomb,
May the morn in heaven awake us,
  Clad in bright, eternal bloom.

197. O Thou God of My Salvation.

C. C. CONVERSE, by per.

1 Oh, thou God of my salvation,
  My Redeemer from all sin!
Moved by thy divine compassion,
  Who hast died my heart to win,
    I will praise thee:
  Where shall I thy praise begin?

2 Though unseen, I love the Savior;
  He hath brought salvation near—
Manifests his pardoning favor;
  And when Jesus doth appear,
    Soul and body
  Shall his glorious image bear.

3 Angels now are hov'ring round us,
  Unperceived amid the throng,
Wond'ring at the love that crowned [us,
  Glad to join the holy song:
    Hallelujah!
  Love and praise to Christ belong.

198. Security of Zion.

1 Zion stands with hills surrounded,
  Zion, kept by power divine;
All her foes shall be confounded,
  Tho' the world in arms combine:
    Happy Zion,
  What a favored lot is thine!

2 Every human tie may perish,
  Friend to friend unfaithful prove;
Mothers cease their own to cherish,
  Heaven and earth at last remove;
    But no changes
  Can attend Jehovah's love.

3 In the furnace God may prove thee,
  Thence to bring thee forth more
      bright,
But can never cease to love thee;
  Thou art precious in his sight:
    God is with thee—
  God, thine everlasting light.

199. Revive Us.

1 Savior, visit thy plantation;
  Grant us, Lord, a gracious rain;
All will come to desolation,
  Unless thou return again.
    Lord, revive us;
  All our help must come from thee!

2 Keep no longer at a distance;
  Shine upon us from on high,
Lest for want of thine assistance
  Every plant should droop and die.
    Lord, revive us;
  All our help must come from thee.

Autumn. 8s & 7s. Double.

Memory. 8s & 7s. Double.

200 Jesus Pleading.

1 Jesus, hail! enthroned in glory,
  There forever to abide;
All the heavenly hosts adore thee,
  Seated at thy Father's side.
There for sinners thou art pleading;
  There thou dost our place prepare;
Ever for us interceding,
  Till in glory we appear.

2 Worship, honor, power, and bless-
  Thou art worthy to receive;   [ing,
Loudest praises, without ceasing,
  Meet it is for us to give.
Help, ye bright angelic spirits;
  Bring your sweetest, noblest lays;
Help to sing our Savior's merits;
  Help to chant Immanuel's praise.

201 Persevere.

1 Toil on, teachers! toil on, boldly,
  Labor on, and watch and pray;
Men may scoff and treat you coldly;
  Heed them not, go on your way.
Jesus is a loving master;
  Cease not, then, this work to do;
Cleave to him still closer, faster,
  He will own and honor you.

2 Toil on, teachers! earnest, steady,
  Sowing well the seeds of truth;
Always willing, cheerful, ready,
  Watching, praying, for your youth.
Patient, firm, and persevering,
  Leaning on the promise sure;
Prayer will surely gain a hearing,
  Faithful to the end endure.

202 The Best Friend.

1 One there is, above all others,
  Well deserves the name of Friend;
His is love beyond a brother's,
  Costly, free, and knows no end.
Which of all our friends to save us,
  Could, or would, have shed his
But our Jesus died to have us [blood?
  Reconciled, in him, to God.

2 When he lived on earth so lowly,
  Friend of sinners was his name;
Now enthroned among the holy,
  He rejoices in the same.
Oh, for grace our hearts to soften!
  Teach us, Lord, at length to love;
We, alas! forget too often
  What a friend we have above.

203 Send Me.

1 Hark! the voice of Jesus crying:
  "Who will go and work to-day?
Fields are white and harvest waiting;
  Who will bear the sheaves away?"
Loud and strong the Master calleth,
  Rich reward he offers thee;
Who will answer, gladly saying,
  "Here am I; send me, send me!"

2 Let none hear you idly saying,
  "There is nothing I can do,"
While the souls of men are dying,
  And the Master calls for you.
Take the task he gives you gladly;
  Let his work your pleasure be;
Answer quickly when he calleth,
  "Here am I; send me, send me!"

204. Watch and Pray.

FANNY CROSBY.   T. E. PERKINS, by per.

1 Softly, on the breath of evening,
Comes the tender sigh of day;
Lonely heart, by sorrow laden,
'Tis the time to pray.

CHORUS.
Weary pilgrim, cease thy mourning,
Weary pilgrim, cease thy mourning,
Rest beyond forever.

2 'Tis the hour when hallowed feelings
Chase our doubts and fears away;
'Tis the hour for calm devotion;
Pilgrim, watch and pray.

3 Tho' temptations dark oppress thee,
Jesus guides thee on thy way;
He will hear thy lightest whisper;
Pilgrim, watch and pray.

Cleansing Wave.

MRS. J. F. KNAPP, by per.

205

1 Oh, now I see the crimson wave!
The fountain deep and wide;
Jesus, my Lord, mighty to save,
Points to his wounded side.

CHORUS.
The cleansing stream, I see, I see!
I plunge, and oh, it cleanseth me!
Oh, praise the Lord! it cleanseth me;
It cleanseth me—yes, cleanseth me.

2 I rise to walk in heaven's own light,
Above the world of sin, [white,
With heart made pure and garments
And Christ enthroned within.

3 Amazing grace! 'tis heaven below
To feel the blood applied;
And Jesus, only Jesus, know,
My Jesus crucified.

206

1 There is a fountain filled with blood,
Drawn from Immanuel's veins,
And sinners, plunged beneath that
Lose all their guilty stains. [flood,

2 Dear dying Lamb, thy precious
Shall never lose its power, [blood
Till all the ransomed Church of God
Are saved to sin no more.

3 E'er since, by faith, I saw the stream
Thy flowing wounds supply,
Redeeming love has been my theme,
And shall be till I die.

4 Then in a nobler, sweeter song,
I'll sing thy power to save,
When this poor lisping, stammering
Lies silent in the grave. [tongue

207. Whosoever Will May Come.

"The Spirit and the Bride say, come."

T. C. O'KANE.

1 Come, ye sinners, poor and needy,
  Weak and wounded, sick and sore;
Jesus ready stands to save you,
  Full of pity, love, and power.
CHORUS.
" *Whosoever,*" *saith the Spirit,*
  With the Father and the Son;
" *Whosoever,*" *sinner, hear it,*
  " *Whosoever will may come.*"

2 Now, ye needy, come and welcome,
  God's free bounty glorify;
True belief and true repentance,
  Every grace that brings you nigh.

3 Let not conscience make you linger,
  Nor of fitness fondly dream;
All the fitness he requireth
  Is to feel your need of him.

4 Come, ye weary, heavy-laden,
  Bruised and mangled by the fall;
If you tarry till you're better,
  You will never come at all.

5 Lo! th' incarnate God, ascending,
  Pleads the merit of his blood;
Venture on him,—venture freely;
  Let no other trust intrude.

208. Come to Jesus.

REV. J. H. STOCKTON.

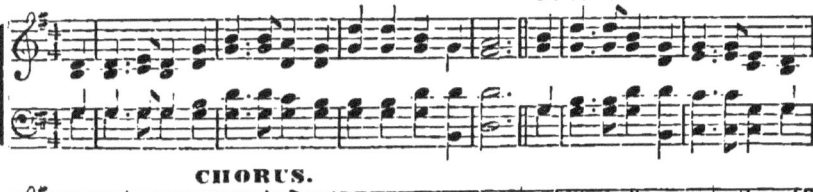

1 Come, trembling sinner, from thy seat,
  And bow before the Lord;
Fall as a mourner at his feet,
  And hang upon his word.
CHORUS.
Come to Jesus, come to Jesus,
  Come to Jesus now;
Only trust him, he will save you,
  He will save just now.

2 Come while you may to Christ and live,
  For life will soon be done;
Oh, come and to the Savior give
  That guilty heart of stone!

3 Come if thou canst, or canst not feel,
  Come trusting in his grace;
He will the work of pardon seal
  On all who seek his face.

4 Come while the voice of Jesus calls,
  In accents full and clear,
And mercy's sweetest language falls
  Inviting on the ear.

5 The Savior stands thy cause to plead
  Before the throne above;
Come in thy hour of greatest need,
  And feel his pard'ning love.

Lenox. H. M.

Carmarthen. H. M.

209   *Our Advocate.*

1 Arise, my soul, arise;
  Shake off thy guilty fears;
  The bleeding sacrifice
    In my behalf appears:
Before the throne my surety stands,
My name is written on his hands.

2 He ever lives above
  For me to intercede,
  His all-redeeming love,
    His precious blood to plead;
His blood atoned for all our race,
And sprinkles now the throne of grace.

3 The Father hears him pray,
  His dear anointed one;
  He can not turn away
    The presence of his Son:
His Spirit answers to the blood,
And tells me I am born of God.

4 My God is reconciled;
  His pard'ning voice I hear;
  He owns me for his child;
    I can no longer fear:
With confidence I now draw nigh,
And Father, Abba, Father, cry.

210   *Praising Jesus.*

1 Let earth and heaven agree,
  Angels and men be joined,
  To celebrate with me
    The Savior of mankind:
T' adore the all-atoning Lamb,
And bless the sound of Jesus' name.

2 Jesus! transporting sound!
  The joy of earth and heaven;
  No other help is found,
    No other name is given,
By which we can salvation have;
But Jesus came the world to save.

3 Jesus! harmonious name!
  It charms the hosts above;
  They evermore proclaim,
    And wonder at, his love:
'Tis all their happiness to gaze,—
'T is heaven to see our Jesus' face.

4 Oh, for a trumpet voice!
  On all the world to call,—
  To bid their hearts rejoice
    In him who died for all:
For all, my Lord was crucified;
For all, for all, my Savior died.

Joy to the World.

211   **Over There.**

1 O think of the home over there,
By the side of the river of light,
Where the saints all immortal and fair
Are rob'd in their garments of white.

REF.—*Over there, over there,
O, think of the home over there.*

2 O think of the friends over there,
Who before us the journey have trod,
Of the songs that they breathe on the air,
In their home in the palace of God.

3 My Savior is now over there,
There my kindred and friends are at rest;
Then away from my sorrow and care
Let me fly to the land of the blest.

212   **The Endless Song.**

1 My life flows on in endless song,
Above earth's lamentation;
I catch the sweet, the far off hymn
That hails a new creation.
Thro' all the tumult and the strife
I hear the music ringing;
It finds an echo in my soul—
How can I keep from singing?

2 I lift my eyes; the cloud grows thin,
I see the blue above it;
And day by day this pathway smooths
Since first I learned to love it;
The peace of Christ makes fresh my heart,
A fountain ever springing;
All things are mine since I am his—
How can I keep from singing?

213   **Nearer to Thee.**

1 Nearer, my God, to thee,
Nearer to thee!
E'en though it be a cross
That raiseth me,
Still all my song shall be,
‖: Nearer, my God, to thee. :‖

2 Though like a wanderer,
The sun gone down,
Darkness comes over me,
My rest a stone,
Yet in my dreams I'd be
Nearer, etc.

3 Or if on joyful wing,
Cleaving the sky,
Sun, moon, and stars forgot,
Upward I fly,
Still all my song shall be,
Nearer, etc.

214   **"Washed in the Blood."**

1 Come to the fountain flowing deep and wide,
Flowing for sinners from Immanuel's side,
Rise from 'neath its purple tide, "Washed," etc.

CHO.—*Glory evermore to the dear Redeemer's name,
"Washed in the blood of the Lamb."*

2 Ye who are burdened with a sense of sin,
Feeling its guilt and secret power within,
May be made entirely clean, "Washed," etc.

3 Still flows the fountain ever full and free,
Saving its thousands, even such as we;
And yet thousands more may be "Washed," etc.

215   **Precious Jesus.**

1 O to love thee, precious Jesus,
O to know that thou art mine;
All my heart I give thee, Jesus,
If thou wilt but make it thine.

CHO.—*Precious name, precious name,
Thou art all the world to me,
All of earth, all of heav'n,
All I want I find in thee.*

2 Take my warmest, best affections;
Take my memory, mind, and will;
Then with all thy loving spirit
All my emptied nature fill.

3 O how precious, dear Redeemer,
Is the love that fills my soul!
It is done! the word is spoken!
"Be thou every whit made whole!"

216   **Precious Blood.**

1 The cross! the cross! the blood-stained cross!
The hallow'd cross I see,
Reminding me of precious blood
That once was shed for me.

CHO.—*O the blood! the precious blood!
That Jesus shed for me
Upon the cross in crimson flood,
Just now by faith I see.*

2 A thousand, thousand fountains spring
Up from the throne of God;
But none to me such blessings bring
As Jesus' precious blood.

3 By faith that blood now sweeps away
My sins, as like a flood;
Nor lets one guilty blemish stay;
All praise to Jesus' blood!

Joy to the World.

217   Trusting.

1 I am coming to the cross;
   I am poor, and weak, and blind;
   I am counting all but dross,
   I shall full salvation find.

CHO.—*I am trusting, Lord, in thee,*
   Dear Lamb of Ca'vary;
   Humbly at thy cross I bow,
   Save me, Jesus, save me now.

2 Here I give my all to thee,
   Friends, and time, and earthly store;
   Soul and body, thine to be,—
   Wholly thine for evermore.

3 Jesus comes! He fills my soul!
   Perfected in him I am;
   I am every whit made whole;
   Glory, glory to the Lamb.

218   The Gate Ajar.

1 There is a gate that stands ajar,
   And through its portals gleaming,
   A radiance from the cross afar,
   The Savior's love revealing.

REF.—*O, depth of mercy! can it be*
   That gate was left ajar for me?
   For me, for me?
   Was left ajar for me?

2 That gate ajar stands free for all
   Who seek through it salvation;
   The rich and poor, the great and small,
   Of every tribe and nation.

3 Beyond the river's brink we'll lay
   The cross that here is given,
   And bear the crown of life away,
   And love him more in heaven.

219   Sweet Sound.

1 How sweet the name of Jesus sounds
   In a believer's ear!
   It soothes his sorrows, heals his wounds,
   And drives away his fear.

CHO.—*O how I love Jesus,*
   Because he first loved me;
   How can I forget thee?
   Dear Lord, remember me.

2 It makes the wounded spirit whole,
   And calms the troubled breast;
   'Tis manna to the hungry soul,
   And to the weary rest.

3 Dear Name! the rock on which I build,
   My shield and hiding-place;
   My never-failing treasure, filled
   With boundless stores of grace.

4 I would thy boundless love proclaim
   With every fleeting breath;
   So shall the music of thy name
   Refresh my soul in death.

220   Unwearied earnestness.

1 Father, I stretch my hands to thee;
   No other help I know;
   If thou withdraw thyself from me,
   Ah! whither shall I go?

CHO. *I do believe, I will believe,*
   That Jesus died for me,
   And on the cross he shed his blood,
   From sin to set me free.

2 Author of faith! to thee I lift
   My weary, longing eyes:
   O let me now receive thy gift,—
   My soul without it dies.

3 Surely thou canst not let me die
   O speak, and I shall live;
   And here I will unwearied lie,
   Till thou thy Spirit give.

221   Leaving All for Jesus.

1 Sad and weary with my longing
   Filled with shame because of sin,
   As I am in conscious weakness,
   Here I must salvation win.

CHO.—*All I have I leave for Jesus,*
   I am counting it but dross;
   I am coming to the Master,
   I am clinging to the Cross.

2 O the joy of knowing Jesus!
   It is dawning on my soul;
   I am finding his salvation,
   And the power that makes me whole.

3 O refine me by thy Spirit!
   Make my earthly life sublime
   With my heart a home for Jesus,
   Till I've done with earth and time.

222   Yielding.

1 And can I yet delay
   My little all to give?
   To tear my soul from earth away
   For Jesus to receive?

CHO.—*I am coming, Lord,*
   Coming now to thee;
   Wash me, cleanse me in the blood
   That flowed on Calvary.

2 Nay, but I yield, I yield;
   I can hold out no more:
   I sink, by dying love compell'd,
   And own thee conqueror.

3 Though late, I all forsake;
   My friends, my all, resign:
   Gracious Redeemer, take, O take,
   And seal me ever thine.

4 C me, and posses me whole,
   Nor hence again remove;
   Settle and fix my wav'ring soul
   With all thy weight of love.

Joy to the World.

223   **Shining Shore.**

1 My days are gliding swiftly by,
   And I, a pilgrim stranger,
Would not detain them as they fly,
   These hours of toil and danger.
Cho.—*For now we stand on Jordan's strand,
Our friends are passing over;
And just before the shining shore
We may almost discover.*

2 We'll gird our loins, my brethren dear,
   Our heavenly homes discerning;
Our absent Lord has left us word,
   Let every lamp be burning.

3 Let sorrow's rudest tempest blow,
   Each cord on earth to sever,
Our King says come, and there's our home,
   Forever, oh, forever!

224   **Sweet Home.**

1 'Mid scenes of confusion and creature complaints,
How sweet to my soul is communion with saints;
To find at the banquet of mercy there's room,
And feel in the presence of Jesus at home.
Cho.—*Home, home, sweet, sweet home,
Prepare me, dear Savior, for glory, my home.*

2 Sweet bonds that unite all the children of peace,
And thrice gracious Jesus, whose love can not cease,
Tho' oft from thy presence in sadness I roam,
I long to behold thee in glory at home.

3 Whate'er thou deniest, oh, give me thy grace!
Thy Spirit's sure witness, and smiles of thy face:
Indulge me with patience to wait at thy throne,
And find, even now, a sweet foretaste of home.

4 I long, dearest Lord, in thy beauty to shine,
No more as an exile in sorrow to pine;
But in thy bright image to rise from the tomb,
With glorified millions to praise thee at home.

225   **By and By.**

1 We speak of the realms of the blest,
   That region so bright and so fair,
And oft are its glories confessed—
   But what must it be to be there?
Cho.—*In the sweet by and by,
We shall rest on that beautiful shore.*

2 We speak of its freedom from sin,
   From sorrow, temptation, and care,
From trials without and within,—
   But what must it be to be there!

3 We speak of its service of love,
   The robes which the glorified wear,
The church of the first-born above—
   But what must it be to be there!

4 O Father! 'mid sorrow and woe,
   For heaven our spirits prepare,
And shortly we also shall know,
   And feel what it *is* to be there.

226   **Blessed Union.**

1 Blest be the tie that binds
   Our hearts in Christian love;
The fellowship of kindred minds
   Is like to that above.

2 Before our Father's throne,
   We pour our ardent prayers;
Our fears, our hopes, our aims are one,—
   Our comforts and our cares.

3 We share our mutual woes,
   Our mutual burdens bear;
And often for each other flows
   The sympathizing tear.

227   **Loving Kindness.**

1 Awake, my soul, to joyful lays,
   And sing the great Redeemer's praise:
He justly claims a song from me,
   His loving kindness, O how free!

2 He saw me ruined in the fall,
   Yet loved me notwithstanding all;
He saved me from my lost estate,
   His loving kindness, O how great!

3 Often I feel my sinful heart
   Prone from my Jesus to depart;
But though I have him oft forgot,
   His loving kindness changes not.

228   **All Paid.**

1 I hear the Savior say,
   Thy strength indeed is small;
Child of weakness, watch and pray,
   Find in me thine all in all.
Cho.—*Jesus paid it all,
All to him I owe;
Sin had left a crimson stain:
He washed it white as snow.*

2 For nothing good have I
   Whereby thy grace to claim—
I'll wash my garment white
   In the blood of Calvary's Lamb.

3 When from my dying bed
   My ransomed soul shall rise,
Then "Jesus paid it all"
   Shall rend the vaulted skies.

4 And when before the throne
   I stand in him complete,
I'll lay my trophies down,
   All down at Jesus' feet.

Joy to the World.

229   Trusting in Jesus.

1 *Trusting alone in Jesus,*
  For all of earth and heav'n,
Ever in him abiding,
  Joy unto me is giv'n.—
Pardon for past transgression,
  Hope for the days to come,
Under his kind protection,
  Safely I journey home.
Cho.—*(Repeat first 4 lines.)*

2 Trusting alone in Jesus,
  Naught can the soul molest,
Free from the fear of evil,
  Of every good possessed.
Thus on the Lord relying,
  He surely leads the way
Thro' every earthly shadow,
  Up to the heavenly day.

230   For Jesus.

1 O who'll stand up for Jesus,
  The lowly Nazarene,
And raise the blood-stained banner
  Amid the hosts of sin?

Cho.—*The cross of Christ I'll cherish,*
  Its crucifixion bear;
All hail reproach or sorrow
  If Jesus leads me there.

2 O who will follow Jesus,
  Amid report and shame?
While others shrink and falter,
  Who'll glory in his name?

3 Though fierce may rage the battle,
  And wild the storm may blow,
Though friends may go forever,
  Who will with Jesus go?

4 My all to Christ I've given,
  My talents, time, and voice,
Myself, my reputation,
  His glory is my choice.

231   Trusting Every Day.

1 Simply trusting every day,
  Trusting through a stormy way,
Even when my faith is small—
  Trusting Jesus, that is all.

Cho.—*Trusting him while life shall last,*
  Trusting him till earth is past,
Till within the jasper wall—
  Trusting Jesus, that is all.

2 Brightly doth his Spirit shine
  Into this poor heart of mine;
While he leads I can not fall—
  Trusting Jesus, that is all.

3 Singing if my way is clear;
  Praying if the path is drear;
If in danger, for him call—
  Trusting Jesus, that is all.

232   The Great Physician.

1 The great Physician now is near,
  The sympathizing Jesus;
He speaks the drooping heart to cheer,
  O, hear the voice of Jesus.

Cho.—*Sweetest note in seraph song,*
  Sweetest name on mortal tongue,
Sweetest carol ever sung,
  Jesus, blessed Jesus.

2 Your many sins are all forgiv'n,
  O, hear the voice of Jesus;
Go on your way in peace to heav'n
  And wear a crown with Jesus.

3 All glory to the dying Lamb,
  I now believe in Jesus;
I love the blessed Savior's name,
  I love the name of Jesus.

233   The Old, Old Story.

1 Tell me the old, old story
  Of unseen things above,
Of Jesus and his glory,
  Of Jesus and his love;
Tell me the story simply,
  As to a little child,
For I am weak and weary,
  And helpless and defiled.

2 Tell me the story softly,
  With earnest tones, and grave;
Remember! I'm the sinner
  Whom Jesus came to save;
Tell me the story always,
  If you would really be
In any time of trouble,
  A comforter to me.

3 Tell me the same old story,
  When you have cause to fear
That this world's empty glory
  Is costing me too dear;
Yes, and when that world's glory
  Is dawning on my soul,
Tell me the old, old story;
  "Christ Jesus makes thee whole."

234   More Love to Thee.

1 More love to thee, O Christ,
  More love to thee!
Hear thou the prayer I make,
  On bended knee;
This is my earnest plea,
  More love O Christ, to thee
More love to thee.

2 Once earthly joy I craved,
  Sought peace and rest,
Now thee alone I seek,
  Give what is best:
This all my prayer shall be,
  More love, etc.

3 Then shall my latest breath
  Whisper thy praise,
This be the parting cry
  My heart shall raise,
This still its prayer shall be
  More love, etc.

INDEX OF HYMNS.

BY NUMBERS.

Hymn	No.
Above earth's grief	48
A charge to keep I have	171
Ah, tell me not	20
Alas, and did my	82
All glory and praise	86
All hail the power	71, 160
All praise to the Lamb	110
Am I a soldier	158
And can it be that	122
And can I yet delay	222
And let this feeble	120
Arise, my soul	209
Ashamed to be a	183
Asleep in Jesus	149
As white as snow	9
As pants the heart	75
Awake my soul to	227
Beautiful day, lovely	29
Behold a stranger	54
Behold the throne of grace	174
Blest be the tie	226
By cool Siloam's	157
By thy birth and by thy	156
Burst, ye emerald gates	178
Cast thy bread upon	192
Children of the	181
Christ in me the hope	49
Come, Holy Spirit	151
Come, my soul, thy suit	69
Come, needy sinners	89
Come, thou Almighty King	74
Come, thou fount	191
Come to the fountain	214
Come, trembling sinner	208
Come, ye sinners	207
Come, ye that love the	108
Dear Jesus, I long	125
Depth of mercy	187
Down at the cross where	34
Enthroned is Jesus now	30
Father, I stretch my	220
Father of mercies, in thy	152
From every stormy wind	150
From Greenland's icy	184
From worldly thought	52
Glorious things of thee	94
God is love, his mercy	130
God shall charge his	93
Grace, 't is a charming	170
Great God, attend while	137
Hark, the voice of Jesus	80
Hasten, sinner, to be wise	180
Hear the royal	57
Hear you not the Savior	92
Heavenly Father, grant	190
He leadeth me	76
Holy Bible, book divine	176
Holy Spirit faithful	127
Hope has left me	28
How firm a foundation	87
How happy every child	164
How sweet the name	219
Hundreds of years	19
I am coming to the	217
I am far frae my hame	126
I am saved	15
I am waiting, O my	55
I believe that God in	32
I bring my sins to thee	63
If the way be full of	64
If you can not be a	119
I gave my life for thee	80
I have a Savior	10
I have work enough	62
I heard the voice of	35
I hear the Savior	228
I know not what shall	56
I know that heaven	6
I know that my Redeemer	143
I love thy kingdom	167
I love to tell the story	96
I'm glad salvation	169
I'm not ashamed	156
In a world so full	85
I need thy presence	103
In the cross of Christ	132
In the world ye shall	38
Into the world a light	105
I remember a voice	45
I rest my soul on	188
I saw a way-worn	133
I've found a friend	8
I've reached the land	14
I want a present	16
I was once far away	123
I will sing you a song	107
I will take my cross	21
Jerusalem, the golden	44
Jesus, from whom all	139
Jesus, hail enthroned	200
Jesus, I my cross	193
Jesus, let me cling	7
Jesus, lover of my soul	175
Jesus loves me	99
Jesus, my all to heaven	131
Jesus only	51
Jesus shall reign	136
Jesus, thine all victorious	165
Joy to the world	1
Just as I am	145
Let earth and heaven	210
Let me go	134
Light after darkness	59
Long my spirit pined	97
Lord, I am thine	146
Lord, I hear of showers	66
Lord, we come before	177
Love divine, all love	189
Many souls on life's	58
Methinks I hear	39
Mid scenes of confusion	224
Mighty rock, whose	2
More love to thee	234
Must Jesus bear	153
My country, 't is of thee	128
My days are gliding	223
My faith looks up	73
My God, the Spring	166
My latest sun is	36
My life flows on	212
My path is dark	24
My soul, be on thy guard	173
Nearer, my God, to thee	213
No, not despairingly	17
Nothing but leaves	25
O Christ, thou art my	124
Of Him who did	138
O for a closer walk	155
O for a faith that	161
O for a heart to	162
O for a thousand tongues	159
O how happy are they	101
O how sweet the name	18
O let us praise	4
O Lord, thy work revive	168
One by one the bonds	31
One, there, is above all	202
O, now I see the	205
On the cross the Savior's	104
On the rock of ages	61
O sometimes the shadows	84
O spirit of the	140
O think of the home	211
O thou, in whose	102
O thou God of my	197
O thou, to whose all	141
O that my load of	148
O to do something	12
O to love the precious	215
Out of darkness	53
O who is like Jesus	109
O who'll stand up	230
Passing Lord by vale	65
Rise, my soul, and stretch	47
Rock of Ages, cleft for me	185
Sad and weary with my	221
Savior, breathe an	196
Savior, visit thy	199
See on the mountain top	40
Shall we gather at	27
Should the death angel	88
Silently the shades	195
Silent night	91
Simply trusting every	231
Softly on the breath	204
Sons of God, your	179
Sowing the seed by the	77
Sow in the morn thy seed	172
Suffering Savior with	13
Sun of my soul	142
Sweet hour of prayer	78
Sweet the moments rich	194
Take the world, but	33
Tell me the old, old	233
The blood of Jesus	105
The cross, the cross	216
The golden sun is	60
The great physician	232
The light of truth is	117
The Lord is my light	95
The morning light is	182
The prize is set before	111
There are songs of joy	72
There is a fountain filled	206
There is a gate that	218
There is a land of	163
There is a spot to me	41
There's a fountain	90

127

INDEX OF HYMNS—CONTINUED.

There's a home for the....	22	Wake from intemperance	116	When all thy mercies......	154
There's a land far away..	83	Wand'rer o'er life's...........	113	When I can read my.........	37
There's not a bright and..	23	Watchman, tell us...........	46	When marshaled on.........	129
There were ninety and......	26	We are toiling up the.......	43	When the cares of life......	70
Tho' the night be dark......	113	We have no outward........	147	When we reach the..........	114
Thou, my everlasting......	115	We praise thee, O God......	5	While we bow in thy........	100
Thus far the Lord............	144	We shall meet beyond.....	68	Will you come..................	11
Till I learned to love........	50	We speak of the realms.....	225	Work for the night is.......	135
To-day the Savior calls....	79	What a friend we have.....	98	Wouldst thou find............	3
Toil on, teachers..............	201	What means this eager.....	112	Yes, I do believe...............	42
Trusting alone in Jesus....	229	What memories are..........	67	Zion stands with..............	198
Vain, delusive world.........	121	What though before me...	81		

INDEX ÷ OF ÷ TUNES.

BY PAGES.

All for Me.........................	13	Hold the Light up Higher	52	Retreat............................	105
All Tears..........................	42	Horton.............................	113	Rockingham...................	105
America...........................	99	Hursley...........................	104	Say, are you Ready........	74
Amsterdam.....................	41	I am Saved.....................	15	Satisfied By and by........	28
And can it Be..................	95	I am the Light................	24	Silent Night....................	77
Anchored Fast................	55	I Believe.........................	30	Siloam.............................	107
Arlington........................	104	I do Believe the Savior....	38	So I can Wait..................	7
As Pants the Hart............	66	It is Good to be Here.......	82	Something for Jesus.......	12
Assurance.......................	84	I've Found a Friend........	9	Song Memories...............	60
As White as Snow...........	10	Jerusalem the Golden.....	39	Steer Straight for Me......	40
Autumn...........................	119	Jesus all the Time...........	43	Stowell............................	117
Azmon.............................	107	Jesus' Blood....................	85	St. Thomas.....................	110
Bartimeus.......................	100	Jesus of Nazareth...........	89	Strike for the Victory.....	92
Beulah Land...................	14	Jesus Only......................	45	Thatcher.........................	111
Beautiful Day..................	27	Jesus Reigns...................	51	The Beloved...................	83
Carmarthen....................	122	Jesus will Give you Rest...	11	The Hallowed Spot.........	37
Cleansing Wave..............	120	Kynett.............................	79	The Joy of Service..........	97
Cleft for Me.....................	4	Laban..............................	111	The Lord is Come...........	3
Close to Thee..................	91	Lamb of Calvary.............	65	The Lord is my Light......	80
Come closer, Soul, to Me..	35	Leaving all, I follow Thee	21	The Mercy-seat..............	46
Come to Jesus.................	121	Lenox..............................	122	The New Song................	64
Coronation.....................	108	Let me Cling to Thee......	8	The Old, Old Story.........	19
Cross and Crown............	106	Light after Darkness.......	53	The Rock that is Higher..	71
Daily Victory..................	16	Linger no Longer............	75	The Standard of the Cross	36
Deliverance will Come...	102	Lord of All.......................	63	The Star of Bethlehem....	100
Disciple...........................	117	Lost and Saved...............	26	The Stranger at the Door	48
Down at the Cross...........	32	Love Divine....................	116	The Voice of Jesus..........	33
Duane Street...................	101	Lovest thou Me...............	93	There'll be Joy By and by	90
Duke Street.....................	103	Martyn............................	112	There's a Land far Away	70
Ere the Sun Goes Down...	56	Merdin............................	113	Thy Light is Come..........	47
Ever Flowing..................	76	Memory...........................	119	To Him be all the Glory...	6
Evergreen Mountains.....	22	Missionary Hymn...........	114	Toplady...........................	115
Follow Me.......................	78	My ain Countrie..............	98	Tribulation......................	34
For Me.............................	69	My all to Thee.................	57	Triumph By and by........	88
From Death unto Life.....	44	My Goal is Christ............	20	Varina.............................	109
Gathering One by One...	29	No Crumb for Me............	59	Waiting for the Light......	49
Give me Jesus.................	31	No, not Despairingly.......	17	Watch and Pray..............	120
Go to Jesus.....................	5	Not Knowing...................	50	Weary Not.......................	58
Guide...............................	99	O how Precious...............	18	Webb...............................	114
Hallelujah I'll Sing..........	87	One Step More................	68	We shall Rest, By and by.	62
Hamburg.........................	104	Only Jesus Crucified.......	94	We're Marching to Zion..	86
Happy Zion.....................	118	Oron................................	41	What of the Night...........	41
Harp................................	108	O thou God of my Salva'n	118	Where are thy Sheaves....	51
Heavenly Shore...............	110	Peoria.............................	109	While the Years are........	72
Heaven Whispers............	23	Prospect..........................	94	Whosoever Will..............	121
Hendon...........................	112	Rathbun..........................	101	Zion.................................	118
He Saves to the Uttermost	96				

www.ingramcontent.com/pod-product-compliance
Lightning Source LLC
Chambersburg PA
CBHW020112170426
43199CB00009B/497